# TORA! TORA!

## Pearl Harbor 1941

## MARK E. STILLE

First published in Great Britain in 2011 by Osprey Publishing,
Midland House, West Way, Botley, Oxford, OX2 0PH, UK
44-02 23rd St, Suite 219, Long Island City, NY 11101, USA
Email: info@ospreypublishing.com
Osprey Publishing is part of the Osprey Group.

A CIP catalog record for this book is available from the British Library.

Print ISBN: 978 1 84908 509 0
PDF e-book ISBN: 978 1 84908 510 6
EPUB e-book ISBN: 978 1 84908 904 3

Page layout by: Bounford.com, Cambridge, UK
Index by Mike Parkin
Typeset in Sabon
Maps by Bounford.com
BEVS by The Black Spot
Originated by United Graphics Pte., Singapore
Printed in China through World Print Ltd.

12 13 14 15 16   11 10 9 8 7 6 5 4 3 2

Osprey Publishing is supporting the Woodland Trust, the UK's leading
woodland conservation charity, by funding the dedication of trees.

www.ospreypublishing.com

## DEDICATION

This book is dedicated to my college professor, Gordon W. Prange,
who remains the preeminent scholar on Pearl Harbor.

## ACKNOWLEDGMENTS

The author is indebted to David Aiken and Alan Zimm, both distinguished
Pearl Harbor experts who graciously reviewed the text and clarified many
points. The author would also like to thank the Yamato Museum for
granting permission to use several photos in the book.

# CONTENTS

# INTRODUCTION

As early as 1914 the Japanese and Americans were thinking of each other as possible future enemies. This potential came more sharply into focus when in the 1930s Japan openly embarked on a path of aggression. Beginning in 1931, Japanese actions clearly indicated that their goal was to dominate East Asia.

The central issue between Japan and the United States in the period leading up to war was Japanese aggression in China. Not only did this aggression threaten China's integrity, but it jeopardized American trade interests. Despite the fact that it was not one of its primary national security interests, the United States remained committed to Chinese sovereignty. As the Japanese pressed deeper into China and prosecuted the war with increasing brutality, the Americans began to translate Japanese dependence on resources from the United States into economic pressure. Throughout 1940 the US ratcheted up the economic pressure on Japan in an attempt to curb Japan's imperial ambitions without war. In July 1941, in an attempt to forestall a Japanese advance into French Indochina, the United States froze all Japanese assets in the United States and slapped Japan with a complete trade embargo including oil. In an era when the US supplied Japan with 75 to 80 percent of its imported oil (and Japan imported 90 percent of all oil that it consumed), this was a declaration of total economic war. Making matters worse for Japan, the governments of Great Britain and the Netherlands followed the lead of the United States.

The hard line pursued by the US demanded a Japanese response. Doing nothing was not an option since within 18 to 24 months Japan's oil supplies would be exhausted, which would reduce it to impotence. Essentially, Japan faced one of two alternatives. It could submit to the United States or seize the initiative and use force to extract itself from this dilemma. The price for submission set by the Americans was too high to contemplate by Japan's military rulers. These demands included that Japan abandon its gains in Indochina, China, and, it was even feared, in Manchuria. Not only was this impossible from the standpoint of national pride, but to do so would place Japan in a permanent position of strategic vulnerability to the United States.

There was little debate within the Japanese leadership that the only alternative was to fight. This course of action offered a way out of the American economic stranglehold since seizure of the lightly defended oil resources in the Dutch East Indies, together with the resources of the British possessions in Asia, could negate the effects of the American embargo. The price of this solution was war with Great Britain and the Netherlands, and, much more importantly, probably with the United States as well. In the minds of the Japanese leadership, all three western powers were linked strategically. Since the Netherlands was already occupied by the Germans, and Great Britain was fighting for its very survival, only the United States possessed the military means to threaten Japan's potential march south.

**DECEMBER 7 1941**

**0600hrs First wave launched**

The driving force behind the Pearl Harbor attack was the commander of the Combined Fleet, Admiral Yamamoto Isoroku. Against almost universal skepticism he achieved his goal of opening the war against the United States with a daring attack against the heart of American naval power. (Naval History and Heritage Command)

With this strategic setting, the Japanese began to look at the best strategy for engaging in a war with the strongest nation and the largest empire on the planet while still fighting a war in China that defied military or political solution. On top of this, Japan still harbored designs of striking the Soviet Union in the Far East. The key for Japan's strategic planners was to gain the six months required to successfully conquer the resource areas in the south to give it the economic base to prosecute a war against all its current and potential enemies.

As dubious as this strategic calculus seemed to any outside observers and even to a few clear-headed Japanese thinkers, Japan now elevated its level of strategic folly by initiating a war against the United States with no clear notion of how such a war might be concluded. This was even more startling when it is remembered that the United States possessed a wide advantage over Japan in every measure of national power. Since Japan's notion of victory over the United States revolved around a negotiated settlement on terms allowing Japan to keep its gains in Asia, the way it began such a war mattered to its outcome. Into this quandary stepped the Imperial Navy, which had been planning a war against its United States counterpart for over 20 years.

To fight a naval war against the United States, the Imperial Navy had been built for a decisive battle near Japanese home waters. With war predicated upon taking and holding key resources areas in Southeast Asia, the Japanese notion of a decisive naval battle was forced to change to reflect the requirement to defend Japan's new gains by mounting a forward defense in the Central and Western Pacific. Now, as war with the United States appeared increasingly certain, Japanese naval strategy was transformed again under the guidance of the commander of the Combined Fleet, Admiral Yamamoto Isoroku. He did not share the almost mythic belief in the decisive battle concept. Yamamoto's key to victory in a war against the United States was a negotiated settlement that would be prompted by an opening blow against the American fleet followed by a quick seizure of the southern resource areas. Under Yamamoto, the Imperial Fleet would not be content to lie in wait for the US Navy as it sailed across the Pacific, but would instead open the war with a crippling blow against the United States Pacific Fleet. So devastating was the blow he was planning that it would shatter US morale and bring the Americans to the negotiating table. This thinking provided the strategic framework for the attack on Pearl Harbor.

# ORIGINS

Throughout 1941, as tension between Japan and the United States mounted, the Japanese pursued a duel track of diplomatic engagement in parallel with preparations for war should negotiations fail. On February 12, 1941, Japan's new ambassador to the United States, Nomura Kichisaburo, presented his credentials to the American Secretary of State, Cordell Hull. Nomura believed that peace could be preserved by negotiations, and remained ignorant throughout the process that his nation was increasingly intent on war while marginalizing diplomacy. On April 16 Hull presented Nomura with the American government's basis for negotiations. Misunderstanding marked the negotiations from the start as demonstrated by the Japanese response the following month. The Japanese consistently overestimated the willingness of the United States to make concessions. The Americans were negotiating on principle and never detected any movement by the Japanese. Accordingly, diplomacy never gained any traction in the run-up to war. Essentially, Nomura's mission could succeed only if the Americans agreed to Japan's terms.

Japanese aggression continued during negotiations and gave even less space for diplomacy. In March 1941 Japan forced France to accept a Japanese garrison at Saigon in Indochina. After the German invasion of Russia on June 22, which the Japanese expected to end in a quick German victory, the Imperial Army and Navy agreed to focus their attentions on Southeast Asia before turning back to the north to pick up the fruits of a German victory over the Soviet Union. An imperial conference on July 2 confirmed the decision to turn south, but also approved a possible attack on the Soviet Union if the opportunity arose. Negotiations would continue, as would military preparations in case negotiations broke down. This conference essentially sealed Japan's path to war and placed primacy on the military solution.

Later in July, the Japanese declared a joint Franco-Japanese protectorate over Indochina and prepared to occupy key ports and airfields. In response, the United States froze all Japanese assets under its control and declared a total trade embargo. This was followed by British and Dutch embargoes. From July to December 1941 Japan and the United States drove inexorably to war. The United States government made clear its price for ending the trade embargo – Japan must give up its gains not only in Indochina, but also in China. This was a price no militarist Japanese government could seriously contemplate. The basic fact of the matter was that peace with the United States was totally incongruent with Japanese intentions to seize Southeast Asia and to become the dominant power in East Asia.

As the clock ticked, the Imperial Navy demanded on August 16 that hostilities commence by October. Two weeks later, the Imperial Army agreed. On September 3 a liaison conference between the Imperial Army and Navy set the timeline for war. Preparations to attack the United States, Great Britain and the Netherlands were to be completed by the last ten days of October. Diplomacy was given until then to meet Japanese demands, after which the decision would be made to commence hostilities.

The cabinet agreed on this timeline the next day. On September 5 a draft of the decision was submitted to the emperor for his review before an imperial conference scheduled for the next day. He did not like the emphasis on military over diplomatic means and promised to question the Army and Navy chiefs of staff at the conference. This unprecedented move was avoided when the prime minister arranged for the emperor to question the service chiefs privately on the afternoon of September 5. In the ensuing exchange the emperor made both promise that they were committed to a diplomatic solution. On the following day, at the full conference, the emperor again made clear his desire to resort to military operations only after all diplomatic means had been exhausted. However, he did not overrule the results of the decision to go to war.

As has already been outlined, there was little room for serious negotiations. Failing progress on the diplomatic front, the Japanese accelerated preparations for war. In late October the emperor was made aware of the planned attack

The day after the attack, President Franklin Roosevelt delivered an address in a joint session of the Senate and House of Representatives requesting a declaration of war against Japan. The ultimate price paid by the Japanese for their relatively minor military gains provided by the Pearl Harbor attack was to provide Roosevelt a solution for his problem of how to bring a divided United States into the war. (Naval History and Heritage Command)

on Pearl Harbor and on November 15 Imperial Headquarters explained to him Phase One of the impending war. Finally, the imperial conference on December 1 confirmed the final decision for war. By this point, the Pearl Harbor attack force was already at sea.

The Pearl Harbor strike was only one of a series of synchronized attacks across the Pacific. Preceding all of this was a planned final communication with the United States government breaking off negotiations. This would be delivered at 1300hrs Washington time on December 7. This was 0730hrs in Honolulu. With the attack scheduled to begin at 0800hrs, it left no room for any delay or problems if the note was to be delivered before hostilities were initiated.

In retrospect, it is clear that diplomacy had no real chance to succeed. Additionally, against this backdrop of diplomatic crisis, the Japanese felt they had to act quickly or the window for selecting a military option would for ever pass them by. On July 19, 1940 the United States Congress passed the Two-Ocean Naval Expansion Act. Once the ships funded in this bill had been constructed, the Imperial Navy would be reduced to a level below that considered essential by the Japanese to prosecute a naval war against the United States. Because the Americans had never seen a need to build up to their treaty limitations through the 1930s, in 1941 the Imperial Navy stood at some 70 percent of the total tonnage of the US Navy. When the US Navy's responsibilities in the Atlantic were considered (and these were growing as the Germans threatened the trade lanes to Europe), the Japanese actually possessed an overall numerical advantage in the Pacific. The Imperial Navy would never be in a more favorable position than it was during 1941.

Aware that it was in a period of relative strength compared to the US Navy, the Imperial Navy began a full mobilization in June 1940. This was a process that would take 18 months to prepare, making the fleet ready for action in December 1941. This was so successful that by that time only a single destroyer remained in overhaul. However, such a high state of readiness could not be maintained long and the large segment of the Japanese merchant fleet converted for military use could not be taken out of commercial use indefinitely.

Meanwhile, as events in Europe unfolded, the US Navy was forced to adjust its deployment. Previously, the great bulk of the US Navy had been stationed in the Pacific to confront the potential Japanese threat. In summer of 1940, with Great Britain's fortunes at a low ebb, the Pacific Fleet was forced to send three battleships, one carrier, four light cruisers, 17 destroyers, three oilers, three transports, and ten auxiliaries to the Atlantic. This movement was known to the Japanese, and placed the Pacific Fleet in a numerically inferior position to the Japanese Combined Fleet. This, and the immense logistical difficulties precluding the Pacific Fleet from moving west, meant that the Americans were in no position to initiate immediate offensive operations in response to Japanese aggression in Southeast Asia. Had clearer minds in Japan prevailed, and had the Japanese understood the Americans' logistical constraints, Japan would have realized that these constraints obviated the need for the Pearl Harbor attack altogether.

**DECEMBER 7 1941**

**0645hrs USS *Ward* sights and attacks submarine; first radar contact on Japanese first wave**

# INITIAL STRATEGY

## The Great All-out Battle Strategy

The Imperial and United States navies had been planning for a naval war against each other since the 1920s. Because of its inferior industrial capacity, combined with the restrictions of the Washington and London naval treaties, the Imperial Navy was in a position of continual inferiority if the total strengths of both navies were compared. Accordingly, in the minds of Japanese strategists, a future naval war in the Pacific would unfold along the following lines. In the initial phase of the conflict, American bases in the Philippines would be neutralized and the Philippines captured. In response, the US Fleet would move from its bases in the Central Pacific (Hawaii) into the Western Pacific to engage the Japanese fleet. The Japanese anticipated that this final clash would take place in the area of the Bonin Islands. In response, the Japanese developed a carefully choreographed campaign to attrite the US Navy and ensure that the ultimate clash would be fought on equal terms where superior Japanese tactics and training would prevail. The battle would start as soon as the American fleet left its base at Hawaii. At this point, Japanese submarines would begin the battle. As the US Fleet approached the Japanese-controlled islands in the Mandates, long-range aircraft would attack.

When the fleets met, the battle would be opened by carriers operating in advance of the main Japanese fleet. These carriers would operate in divisions (two carriers), not massed, and their target was to strike the American carriers, which would have the effect of denying the Americans air cover. Before the battle fleets clashed, mixed combat groups would attack the American battle line to cripple it in advance of the climactic gun duel between dreadnoughts. It was envisioned that these groups would attack at night. Holes in the American screening force would be opened by Japanese fast battleships and heavy cruisers, and then the heavy cruisers with their powerful torpedo armament would be joined by destroyer squadrons to launch massed torpedo attacks. These attacks would account for approximately a third of the American fleet and also destroy its cohesion.

The next day, the Japanese battle fleet would join for the *coup de grâce*. Japanese battleships were built to maximize their firepower and range, and it was believed that these advantages would translate into a crushing defeat for the Americans. This was known as the Great All-out Battle strategy and was the strategy with which the Imperial Navy prepared for war, and for which it was trained and equipped. It was never tested in an actual fleet exercise, but it was the holy grail of Japanese strategists. The decisive battle itself replaced the need for planning a real campaign against a modern opponent.

## Yamamoto Enters the Picture

Imperial Navy strategy began to change when Yamamoto took command of the Combined Fleet in August 1939. He turned long-standing Japanese naval dogma on its head and became the originator and chief advocate for the Pearl Harbor operation. He was a complex figure, but was surely not the advocate for peace portrayed by many historians. Yamamoto was an ardent nationalist raised in the samurai tradition. He supported the notion that Japan should establish hegemony over Asia, and as war loomed in 1941 he also supported the idea that Japan would have to go to war to save its empire and its very existence. Thus, he supported the proposed attack to seize the southern resource areas. The dilemma for Yamamoto was that he, like almost all Japanese strategists, believed that initiating a war with Great Britain and the Netherlands to seize their Far Eastern possessions would inevitably lead to a war with the United States as well. This fatal assumption, probably incorrect, led Yamamoto to employ his instincts for boldness and risk to find a way to deal with the US at the start of the conflict. Yamamoto had lived in the United States and was educated at Harvard. This gave him an understanding of the military and technological advantages enjoyed by the United States as well as its immense industrial capacities. However, he failed to understand the degree of difficulty which any US government would face in mobilizing the American population for war, especially if direct American interests were not at stake. Thus, Yamamoto set on a course to solve the Roosevelt administration's most vexing problem.

After assuming command of the Combined Fleet, Yamamoto acquiesced with the Naval General Staff's change of location for the Great All-out Battle from the Bonins and Marianas eastward to the Carolines and Marshalls. As this was occurring, the United States moved the Pacific Fleet from the West Coast to Pearl Harbor in May 1940. This was intended to deter future Japanese aggression. To Yamamoto it was clearly a threat, and eventually an opportunity.

There is a long history of both American and Japanese naval thinkers and strategists considering the possibility of an air attack on Pearl Harbor. As early as 1927, war games at the Japanese naval war college included a raid against Pearl Harbor with two carriers. The following year, senior Imperial Navy officers lectured on the same subject and a certain Captain Yamamoto lectured the torpedo establishment on the same. A practical demonstration of the suitability of carrier air power for such an attack was provided in 1929 when two American carriers conducted a surprise attack

DECEMBER 7
1941

0702hrs
Opana radar
station picks up
aircraft 130 miles
north of Oahu

DECEMBER 7
1941

0715hrs
Second wave
launched

on the Panama Canal in a widely publicized annual fleet exercise. In 1936 the Japanese naval war college again explored the possibility and in 1938 the annual US Fleet exercise featured an attack on Pearl Harbor by a carrier. Authors also toyed with the notion, including a Japanese writer in 1933 and the famous American Hector Bywater in his 1925 book *The Great Pacific War*.

## An Idea is Born

The driving force behind the Pearl Harbor attack was Yamamoto. According to his chief of staff, Vice Admiral Shigeru Fukudome, Yamamoto first mentioned the plan to attack Pearl Harbor in March or April 1940. The idea again surfaced during the late fall of 1940 when, after the completion of the Combined Fleet's annual maneuvers, Yamamoto told Fukudome of his desire to have Rear Admiral Takijiro Onishi study a Pearl Harbor attack under the utmost secrecy. Thus, the conceptual framework of an attack on Pearl Harbor launched from carriers was ingrained in Yamamoto's mind in 1940. After the attack, he wrote to a fellow admiral and friend that he had decided to launch such an attack in December 1940. If this is to be believed, and there is no reason to doubt Yamamoto in this regard, he had decided on a risky course of action before it was even determined whether such an operation was technically feasible, and before the benefits of such an operation had been weighed. This takes the Hawaii operation from the realm of visionary to foolhardy. Even more importantly, it raises the question of why Yamamoto was deciding Japan's overall war plans since this was the prerogative of the Naval General Staff, not that of the supposedly subordinate Combined Fleet and its commander.

One thing is clear, the idea of an attack on Pearl Harbor did not spring into Yamamoto's mind after he learned of the Royal Navy attack against the Italian fleet anchorage at Taranto on November 12, 1941. This attack put three Italian battleships out of action for varying periods (one permanently) and did feature the use of torpedoes in a shallow water harbor. But Yamamoto was thinking much bigger than the one carrier and 21 aircraft used by the British. As the premier practitioners of carrier air power, the Imperial Navy had very little to learn from the British.

# EARLY PLANNING

With the vision of the attack in his head, Yamamoto proceeded to explore how such an attack could be carried out. It should be pointed out that at this stage the attack was not a foregone conclusion because of many important technical and planning factors which remained to be overcome. In a letter dated January 7, 1941 Yamamoto ordered Rear Admiral Takijiro Onishi to study the proposal. This letter was followed by a meeting between Yamamoto and Onishi on January 26 or 27 during which Yamamoto explained his vision. Onishi was the chief of staff of the land-based 11th Air Fleet but was a fellow air advocate and a noted tactical expert and planner.

In February, Onishi pulled Commander Genda Minoru into the planning. Genda was shown Yamamoto's letter; his initial reaction was that the operation would be difficult, but not impossible. He agreed with Onishi that secrecy was an essential ingredient of planning and that the operation needed to include all available carriers to guarantee success. Genda immediately aborted any consideration of making the attack a one-way mission to reduce the exposure of the carriers and he expanded the scope of the attack from just an attack by torpedo bombers. Onishi charged Genda with completing his study of the proposed operation in seven to ten days. In his ensuing report, Genda presented what he considered to be the keys to success. The main elements of the report are detailed here since the final plan reflected much of Genda's early thinking.

1. Surprise was a prerequisite
2. The main objective of the attack was the Pacific Fleet's carriers
3. American land-based air power on Oahu needed to be destroyed
4. Every Japanese carrier with sufficient range needed to be employed in the operation
5. The attack would include not just torpedo bombing, but level- and dive-bombing
6. A strong fighter escort was needed
7. The attack would be mounted early in the morning
8. Refueling was necessary
9. All planning had to be conducted in strict secrecy

**DECEMBER 7 1941**

**0735hrs Scout plane from cruiser *Chikuma* reports Pacific Fleet in harbor**

Genda was to become the driving force behind the attack, second only to Yamamoto himself. On about March 10, Onishi presented an expanded draft of Genda's plan to Yamamoto and included his own thoughts. Ironically, while originally optimistic about the proposed attack, Onishi later began to discount the viability of such a risky venture.

On April 10, 1941 the Imperial Navy took a revolutionary step and formed the First Air Fleet by combining the First and Second Carrier Divisions, along with their escorting destroyers, into a single formation. This step had been debated within the Imperial Navy for some time, but now Yamamoto judged the time was right. The commonly held perception was that carriers were very vulnerable to air attack. If detected, their destruction was considered likely; if all the carriers were placed in a single force, the entire air power of the Imperial Navy would be at risk. Previous Imperial Navy doctrine had dictated that carriers operate in divisions, reducing the risk of simultaneous detection and destruction. The cost of this dispersal, however, was an inability to mass airpower. The advocates of concentration pointed out that massing several carriers into a single force did not increase their vulnerability, but increased their defensive powers by concentrating the numbers of escort ships and defensive fighters. The biggest advantage was the ability to increase the offensive punch of the carriers themselves. This was an important step because without the First Air Fleet the Hawaii operation would not have been possible. It was also to become the focal point for operational planning for the attack.

While planning continued on the Hawaii operation, Yamamoto began to take steps to sell the concept to the Naval General Staff and in late April the process of negotiation began. Yamamoto entrusted the eccentric but brilliant Captain Kuroshima Kameto from his staff with the task of convincing the skeptical Naval General Staff. The first meeting did not go well. Kuroshima explained Yamamoto's basis for the plan, which was to strike first to gain the initiative so that the Japanese would gain the unhindered six months to complete the conquest of the southern resource areas. In Yamamoto's mind, the attack would be so devastating that it would not only militarily cripple the Americans, but undermine their morale. The Naval General Staff were not impressed and thought the plan to be too risky. Their focus was on the southern operation, and they believed the carriers of the First Air Fleet were required to complete the operation quickly. However, on April 10, Admiral Nagano Osami took over the Naval General Staff. He proved no match for the energetic and forceful Yamamoto, and though he could have asserted his control over his impetuous subordinate, he never even tried to do so.

Also in late April, the staff of the new First Air Fleet was pulled into the planning. The first to be officially informed was chief of staff Rear Admiral Kusaka Ryunosuke. When Kusaka outlined the plan to his boss, Vice Admiral Chuichi Nagumo,

Admiral Nagano Osami, head of the Naval General Staff, was nominally Yamamoto's superior officer. However, he proved no match for the energetic Yamamoto in the planning process during the period leading to war. Ultimately, Yamamoto's threat to resign translated into permission to execute his risky Pearl Harbor attack. This was not the last time Yamamoto used this tactic; the same method was employed to gain permission to execute his Midway operation. (Naval History and Heritage Command)

his first thoughts were that the problem with refueling and the unlikelihood of arriving off Pearl Harbor undetected made the plan impossible. These doubts translated to Kusaka the more he thought about it. Thus, ironically, the admirals with the most doubt about the plan were those also charged with its execution. One member of the First Air Fleet staff had no doubts though. This was Genda, who was now assigned as staff air officer. It now fell upon him to continue planning.

## Combined Fleet vs. Naval General Staff

The campaign to convince the Naval General Staff resumed on August 7 when Kuroshima returned to Tokyo to plead Yamamoto's case. He requested that the annual war games be held in September in order to leave time for the Combined Fleet to absorb any lessons, and that they include a realistic examination of the Pearl Harbor plan. With the recent American trade embargo and the need for a response in mind, the Naval General Staff gave Yamamoto's plan another look; while they agreed to include the Hawaii operation in the annual war games, they did not see Yamamoto's plan as any less risky. They again pointed out to Kuroshima that the plan depended on a combination of gaining surprise, developing refueling techniques, and developing adequate torpedo- and level-bombing experience to deliver sufficient air power to guarantee results. The Naval General Staff clung to the belief that a major fleet clash in the area of the Marshall Islands would develop to Japan's favor, making the risky Pearl Harbor attack unnecessary. Kuroshima admitted that the plan was "an adventurous operation" but still advocated it powerfully. Again, the plan survived contact with the Naval General Staff as officers there did not take it directly to Nagano to gain his veto.

In early September the staff of the First Air Fleet was directed by Kusaka to commence the creation of an operational plan for the Pearl Harbor attack. Genda was put in charge of the effort but Kusaka reserved the vexing problem of refueling for himself. Genda gave careful consideration to the question of the best route for the Japanese strike force to take to Hawaii. Though a southern and central route offered less stringent fuel requirements, Genda recommended and Kusaka approved the northern approach. In spite of the rough weather, which made refueling more difficult, and the greater distance, which made multiple refueling necessary, this route offered the greatest prospect for gaining the all-important element of surprise. Nagumo had to be convinced, as he favored the easier southern route through the Marshall Islands since he already assumed that surprise was impossible.

The annual war games began on September 11 at the Imperial Naval Staff College in Tokyo. The first phase lasted through September 16 and focused on a rehearsal of the southern operation. On September 16 a select group of officers vetted by Yamamoto began a study of the Hawaii operation. Among the invitees were representatives of the Naval General

Vice Admiral Chuichi Nagumo was appointed commander of the First Carrier Striking Force in April 1941. Ironically, though charged to lead Yamamoto's bold Hawaii operation, he doubted its success throughout its planning and execution. (Naval History and Heritage Command)

N

| | |
|---|---|
| 🦅 | Radar site |
| ■ | Military base |
| ● | Airfield |

0  2  4  6  8  10km
0     2     4     6 miles

*Kahuku Point*

Waialee

🦅 Opana Radar Site

Kahuku ●

Laie ●

🦅 Kawailda Radar Site

*Waialua Bay*

*Kaena Point*

● Haleiwa Field

Waialua

*K O O L A U*

Kaawa Radar Site 🦅

*Kualoa Point*

Schofield Barracks ■

Waikane ●

*Kaneohe Bay*

NAS Kaneohe Bay ●

*Mokapu Point*

● Wheeler Field

*R A N G E*

*W A I A N A E   R A N G E*

*Kailua Bay*

● Waianae

Pearl City ●    Heeia ●

Ford Island NAS Pearl Harbor ●

Fort Shafter ■

Waimanalo ●

🦅 Fort Shafter Radar Site

Ewa ●    Fort Weaver ■

Hickam Field ●

Bellows Field ●

● Ewa Marine Corps Air Station

■ Fort Kamehameha

Honolulu ●

*Sand Island*

Fort Armstrong

*Makapuu Point*

*Barbers Point*

■ Fort Derussy

Fort Ruger ■

*Mamala Bay*

*Maunalua Bay*

🦅 Koko Head Radar Site

*Diamond Head*

*Koko Head*

---

**Haleiwa Field**
47th Pursuit Squadron (subordinate to 15th Pursuit Group based at Wheeler)

**Bellows Field**
44th Pursuit Squadron (subordinate to 18th Pursuit Group; 10–12 fighters present on December 7)
86th Observation Squadron
2x OA-9, 7x O-47B, 1x B-18
Note: prior to December 7, the 47th Pursuit Squadron (Fighter) and the 44th Pursuit Squadron (Interceptor) were deployed to Haleiwa and Bellows Field, respectively, for gunnery practice. Because aircraft may have flown back and forth to Wheeler over the weekend preceding the attack, the exact number and types of aircraft actually located at Haleiwa and Bellows cannot be determined.

**Wheeler Field**
14th Pursuit Wing with 15th and 18th Pursuit Groups
12x P-40C, 87x P-40B, 39x P-36A, 6x P-26A, 6x P-26B, 3x B-12A, 4x AT-6, 3x OA-9, 1x OA-8

**Ewa Marine Corps Air Station**
Marine Air Group 21 (VMF-211, VMSB-232, VMJ-252)
8x SB2U-3, 23x SBD-1/2, 10x F4F-3, 1x SNJ-3, 2x J2F-4, 1x JO-2, 1x JRS-1, 2x R3D-2

**NAS Kaneohe Bay**
Patrol Wing 1 (VP-11, VP-12, VP-14)
36x PBY-5 (3 absent on patrol), 1x OS2U

**Hickam Field**
18th Bombardment Wing (Heavy) with 5th and 11th Bombardment Groups
58th Bombardment Squadron (Light)
19th Transport Squadron
12x B-17D, 32x B-18, 12x A-20A, 2x P-26A, 2x A-12, 2x C-33, 1x B-24A
Note: additionally, 8x B-17E and 4x B-17C from 38th and 88th Reconnaissance Squadrons arrived during the attack.

**NAS Pearl Harbor**
Patrol Wing 2 (VP-22, VP-23, VJ-2)
13x PBY-3, 12x PBY-5, 4x PBY-1, 1x SOC-1, 1x SU-3, 7x J2F-1/2/3/4
Note: additionally, there were a total of 77 other US Navy aircraft on Oahu. Many (27) were liaison, scout, and transport aircraft based at Pearl Harbor but the majority (50) were battleship and cruiser floatplanes and reserve carrier aircraft based on various ships and at Ford Island.

Primary Defense Installations and Air Order of Battle on Oahu

Staff and Nagumo and his staff. Both would have to be convinced that the operation was feasible. The examination keyed on two major points: was the operation technically feasible, and what were the prospects for surprise? One of the first issues debated was the best route for carriers to take to Oahu. Genda's preferred northern route was supported by most of the other participants, and Nagumo was forced to acquiesce. Another discussion centered on whether reconnaissance aircraft should be flown en route to the target. Genda again got his way when it was decided not to conduct any flight operations because of the potential loss of surprise if there was a mishap.

When the game commenced, the first iteration of the attack was a fiasco for the Japanese. Nagumo's force was discovered before it had a chance to launch its attack. When the attacking aircraft reached Pearl Harbor, they met a determined American defense and inflicted only minor damage. In return, American air raids sank two of Nagumo's four carriers. In the second exercise, Nagumo adjusted his approach track further to the north and modified the time of arrival within the potential American search zone. This time, surprise was assumed and the results were spectacular, with four battleships, two carriers, and three cruisers sunk, and another battleship, a carrier, and three cruisers damaged. Japanese air losses were assessed to be light. When the Americans located Nagumo's force, counterattacks accounted for one Japanese carrier sunk and another damaged. The war games (which in fact had more characteristics of a controlled experiment to examine various courses of action) had shown the operation as feasible, but also seemed to demonstrate the potential risk if surprise was not obtained. The problematic fuel issue was not covered and was pushed over to a future staff study. Also, the question of how many carriers would be allocated to the operation was not decided. The Naval General Staff refused to completely denude the southern operation of carrier air cover, so only three, or a maximum of four, carriers were considered for the Hawaii attack. The entire exercise had taken a day to accomplish, with a second day for critique and discussion of the results.

The exercise had done nothing to change the minds of the Naval General Staff. From Nagano down, the thinking remained that the operation was

*Akagi* was Nagumo's flagship for the operation. It was a converted battlecruiser and embarked 66 aircraft (21 fighters, 18 dive-bombers, and 27 attack planes) for the raid. It was sunk six months later at the battle of Midway. (Naval History and Heritage Command)

DECEMBER 7
1941

0749hrs
Fuchida gives
attack signal

simply too risky. On September 24 the Operations Staff of the Naval General Staff held a conference on the proposed Hawaii attack. Kusaka argued against the attack, and predictably Genda supported it. Kuroshima argued for his boss's plan and when he reported the results of the conference to Yamamoto, the admiral exploded in anger.

As planning continued for the operation, the aviators of the First Air Fleet were solving the problems associated with executing a torpedo attack in the shallow waters of Pearl Harbor and making level bombing a viable tactic. Fueling was the last problem solved. Only seven ships (carriers *Kaga*, *Shokaku*, and *Zuikaku*, along with the two escorting battleships and the two Tone class heavy cruisers) had the radius to make the trip from the Kuriles to Pearl Harbor without refueling. Kusaka arranged that the three shorter-ranged carriers carry extra fuel in 55-gallon drum tanks, and developed and perfected a system allowing the ships to refuel under way. Eight tankers were allotted to support the operation (only seven took part due to problems with one of the ships). Three refueling exercises were held in November and then as the ships of the attack force headed north to the Kuriles all ships took on fuel ten times.

With the technical aspects of the plan addressed, Yamamoto still had to convince his own leaders within the Combined Fleet and on the Naval General Staff that the operation was worth the risk. On October 13 another round of table maneuvers was held on Yamamoto's flagship battleship *Nagato* to refine aspects of the Hawaii operation and to synchronize it with the southern operation. Only three carriers were used, *Kaga*, *Zuikaku*, and *Shokaku* because they had the radius to sail to Pearl Harbor; *Akagi*, *Soryu*, and *Hiryu* were reserved for the southern operation. For the first time, fleet

and midget submarines were included in the planning. The next day there was a review of the event where all admirals present were invited to speak. All but one was opposed to the Hawaii operation. When they were done, Yamamoto addressed the group and declared that as long as he was in charge, Pearl Harbor would be attacked. The time for bickering among the Combined Fleet's admirals was finished.

Now Yamamoto had to quiet the doubts still lingering in the Naval General Staff about his pet plan; Kusaka and Nagumo collaborated to force the issue. Kusaka left *Akagi* on October 17 for Tokyo to vigorously make the case that all six carriers were needed. He was rebuffed again. When word reached Yamamoto, he decided to bring the issue to a head. He sent Kuroshima the following day to gain clarification on the Naval General Staff's view of the operation and to address the carrier allocation issue. Kuroshima was given a powerful weapon to play in the ongoing and seemingly endless debate. Again, as he had in July, Kuroshima outlined his reasons for the attack. Just as adamantly, officers on the Naval General Staff outlined their reasons for opposing it. Now Kuroshima played his ace, revealing that unless the plan was approved in its entirety Yamamoto and the entire staff of the Combined Fleet would resign. This threat immediately changed the entire dynamic of the debate and the Naval General Staff quickly folded. The idea of going to war without Yamamoto at the helm of the Combined Fleet was inconceivable. So Yamamoto got his way, and all six carriers were earmarked for the attack.

On November 3 Nagumo revealed the Pearl Harbor plan to his entire command. Next day a dress rehearsal for the raid was held. Another rehearsal was conducted on November 5. On this occasion, it was simulated that enemy fighters intercepted the attackers 80 miles north of the target. Overall, the results of the drills were disappointing, and the problems with torpedoes diving too deep was still in evidence.

Meanwhile, the timing of the operation was being refined. This was driven by the desire to attack on a Sunday when it was expected that American readiness would be at its lowest. Just as importantly, intelligence reporting indicated that Sunday was the day that the greatest number of Pacific Fleet would be present in harbor. The attack had to be launched in early December, giving the army enough time to complete the conquest of Southeast Asia before the start of the monsoon season due to start in late April. With these requirements in place, Yamamoto's great risk was put into motion.

*Hiryu* was an improved version of *Soryu* and carried an identical air group to *Soryu* for the Pearl Harbor attack (63 aircraft). It too was sunk at Midway. (Yamato Museum)

# THE PLAN

On October 2 Nagumo called the key officers of the First Air Fleet together to share with them the secret of the Hawaii operation. After Nagumo broke the news, Genda described the plan in detail. From now on, in order to accomplish training in the short time remaining, each component air unit would focus on its specific task. Most of the airmen supported the bold plan enthusiastically, and the revelation served to bring a new focus and energy to the task at hand.

## The Training Program

On August 25 Commander Fuchida Mitsuo arrived to take charge of the First Air Fleet's training program. The results were immediate and together Fuchida and Genda began to solve the problems that had mitigated against a successful strike.

One of the most vexing problems was how to use torpedoes in the shallow waters of Pearl Harbor. As early as June, Genda had set the torpedo aviators to an extensive program of torpedo practice under the belief that this was the hardest technique to perfect. A site near Kagoshima on the island of Kyushu was selected for the training because of its similarity to Pearl Harbor.

In October, the most experienced and skilled pilots flying the Type 97 carrier attack plane were selected to train as torpedo bombers; the rest would train in the level-bombing role. Fuchida decided that the torpedo planes would attack in single file, as this was more suited to the geography of Pearl Harbor with its many obstructions. Intensive training resulted in a high percentage of the pilots mastering the art of coming in at low level over land and then settling to a precise altitude to drop their torpedoes.

It was essential to incorporate torpedoes into the attack plan as their ship-killing power was far superior to bombs. The waters of Pearl Harbor were some 40ft deep; usually, when an aircraft dropped a heavy object like a torpedo, it would dive much deeper before adjusting to its pre-set running depth. The Japanese endeavored to ensure that their torpedoes did not dive below 33ft. This was done by modifying the Type 91 air-launched torpedo

This photo, taken from 2,500ft altitude on May 3, 1940, gives a good orientation of the naval base. The view is looking south, toward the harbor entrance. The base is full of ships, much like on the morning of December 7, 1941. There are eight battleships present and the carrier *Yorktown* is tied up by Ford Island, which is located in the center of the harbor. Two more battleships and many cruisers, destroyers, and other ships are also present, most of them moored in groups in the East Loch located in the foreground. In the distance is Hickam Army Airfield. (Naval History and Heritage Command)

with a set of wooden extension fins attached to the torpedo's metal horizontal and vertical fins. The wooden fins stabilized the torpedo after it was dropped, and broke off when entering the water. However, as late as the dress rehearsals in November the torpedoes continued to dive too deep. Almost in desperation, Genda and Lieutenant Commander Murata Shigeharu (the Imperial Navy's foremost aerial torpedo expert) devised another tactic calling for a drop at 65ft at 100 knots using the modified torpedoes. This seemed to do the trick. In a series of tests on November 11–13, aircraft from *Akagi* and *Kaga* were able to achieve a success rate of 83 percent. This was a remarkable achievement and an essential one since the success of the torpedo bombers was critical to the success of the entire operation.

Production of the specially modified torpedoes had to be expedited to meet the attack timelines. By the end of November, the Nagasaki Navy Arsenal had built a total of 120 torpedoes. The first 50 built were allocated to *Akagi*, *Soryu*, and *Hiryu* in mid-November before the carriers moved up to the Kuriles. Another batch of 50 were loaded on *Kaga* but did not arrive at Hitokappu Bay until November 24, just two days before the fleet sailed.

Another challenge was to improve the accuracy of level bombing. This was a key ingredient for success as the Japanese were aware that the typical pattern for the Americans to berth their battleships in Pearl Harbor was to moor them in pairs. This meant that only the outer battleship was vulnerable to torpedo attack. To attack the inner ships, only bombs could be used. The bombs delivered by Japanese dive-bombers were relatively small (250kg) and could not penetrate the decks of a heavily armored ship. The preferred solution was to use horizontal bombers that could carry a much larger bomb.

The problem with horizontal bombing was that it is much less accurate than dive-bombing. This is demonstrated by the fact that prior to April 1941 the Japanese were achieving a hit rate of about 10 percent using this method. Results were so bad that even Genda considered giving up. In April a new technique was introduced by the leader of *Akagi*'s level bombers that

**DECEMBER 7 1941**

**0753hrs Kaneohe Naval Air Station and Ewa Mooring Mast Field attacked**

Zuikaku carried 72 aircraft for the Hawaii operation – 18 fighters, 27 dive-bombers, and 27 attack planes. *Zuikaku* was the last of the Pearl Harbor carriers to be lost, surviving until the battle of Leyte Gulf in October 1944. (Yamato Museum)

This aerial view gives a good perspective of the main facilities located in the Pearl Harbor area. The view was taken on October 30, 1941 and looks to the southwest. Ford Island is in the center of the picture. Across the channel to the left is the Navy Yard; to the left of that is the Submarine Base. Hickam Army Airfield is the large airfield in the upper left of the image. (Naval History and Heritage Command)

revolved around a group of nine aircraft dropping their bombs all at the same time. This mass drop was done at the signal of the lead aircraft in which the pilot and bombardier worked closely together to ensure accuracy. With these improvements, three to five hits were scored out of nine.

To penetrate the deck armor of a battleship, it was calculated that a bomb of 800kg would be required and that it would have to be dropped from an altitude of 10,000–12,000ft. To create such a bomb quickly it was discovered that obsolete 16in shells from the Nagato-class battleships could be modified and converted into bombs with sufficient mass and penetrating power. The bomb was designated Type 99 Model 80-3, which weighed in at 796.9kg with a warhead of 22.8kg. As with the special torpedoes, construction of the new bomb in the numbers desired proved difficult and only 150 were available as of mid-September.

Later in the training program, it was decided by Genda and Fuchida that the level bombers would drop from 3,000m (9,843ft) since this was the minimum altitude required to pierce the battleship's armor but it was low enough to ensure better accuracy. It was later confirmed during tests that bombs dropped from this altitude could penetrate battleship armor. Genda and Fuchida also decided to adopt a five-plane attack section for level bombing, replacing the previous nine-plane group. This gave Genda more flexibility in planning his attack.

The carrier dive-bombers carried 250kg bombs that were available in high-explosive and semi-armor-piercing variants. This bomb was thought sufficient to destroy relatively lightly armored aircraft carriers and cruisers. What the dive-bombers lacked in bomb weight they made up for in accuracy. In the second half of 1941, dive-bombers' accuracy rates reached 50 to 60 percent after constant practice. To gain this degree of precision, the crews were led in intensive drills led by Lieutenant Commander Egusa Takashige, recognized as the Imperial Navy's foremost dive-bomber expert. In order to gain greater accuracy, he proposed that each bomber's release point be changed from 600m (1,969ft) to 450m (1,476ft).

Genda also challenged the fighter units of the six carriers to hone their skills. Under Lieutenant Commander Itaya Shigeru from *Akagi* they practiced a range of basic combat skills. One critical skill that had to be developed was navigation over longer distances.

Previously, the Imperial Navy had not sent a fighter unit more than 100 miles from its carrier; to take part in the Pearl Harbor attack the distance to the target would be over twice that. With the addition of the two carriers of the Fifth Carrier Division, the Japanese had significant problems finding sufficient fighter pilots for all six carriers. This was done only by stripping the smaller carriers of the Third and Fourth Carrier Divisions of fighters and by taking the best pilots from the training establishment. These measures resulted in a full load of fighters by November.

## Japanese Air Group Employment

By December 1941 the Japanese had reached a high level of speed and coordination in operating the air groups of the First Carrier Striking Force. The air groups of all six fleet carriers were organized in an identical fashion, though the numbers of aircraft aboard each ship might vary by class. Each air group was an integrated part of the ship's company and contained three squadrons: a fighter squadron equipped with the famous A6M Type 0 carrier fighter; a squadron of carrier bombers equipped with the relatively slow but deadly D3A1 Type 99 dive-bomber; and a squadron of carrier attack planes. This last squadron was equipped with the B5N Type 97 carrier attack plane, which could operate as either a torpedo bomber or a horizontal bomber. Each of the squadrons was composed of a number of nine-plane sections. Typically, fighter squadrons had 18 aircraft. Carrier bomber and attack plane squadrons were composed of either two or three sections, making a total of 18 or 27 aircraft depending on whether the squadron was assigned to the smaller Soryu class or the larger ships of the Shokaku class and the unique *Akagi* and *Kaga*. Additionally, each ship carried a number of reserve aircraft (usually three of each type). In December 1941 the air groups of the First Carrier Striking Force were at full strength. Though sources vary, the Japanese embarked at least 411 aircraft for the operation. This made the First Carrier Striking Force the most powerful naval force on the planet.

When the Japanese employed their air groups, they did so in a way to minimize launch times. Typically, half of the ship's fighters were assigned to escort the attack force and the other half maintained onboard for air defense. Japanese carriers did not operate as single units but as a component of a two-ship carrier division. When launching strikes, both ships of the same division would launch one of their attack squadrons, with escorting fighters, in a single deck load. This made for quick launches. After the first attack group was launched, the aircraft from the second attack squadron would be

*Shokaku* was the flagship of Rear Admiral Hara Chuichi's Fifth Carrier Division. The two ships of this class were the best Japanese carrier designs of the early war period. *Shokaku* carried 72 aircraft for the attack – 18 fighters, and 27 each dive-bombers and attack planes. *Shokaku* was sunk at the battle of the Philippine Sea in June 1944. (Yamato Museum)

OVERLEAF: The two top profiles are Type 0 fighters. The first is that of Lieutenant Commander Itaya, leader of the first wave fighters. The second fighter is from *Shokaku* and was the aircraft of Lieutenant Commander Kaneko Tadashi who attacked Kaneohe Naval Air Station in the first wave. In the middle are two Type 99 carrier bombers. The first is from *Kaga*; the second is from *Zuikaku*. The two bottom profiles are Type 97 carrier attack aircraft. The first one is from *Soryu*; this aircraft conducted a level bombing attack against Battleship Row. The second aircraft is from *Hiryu*. This aircraft was flown by Lieutenant Matsumura Hirata and delivered a torpedo hit against battleship *West Virginia*.

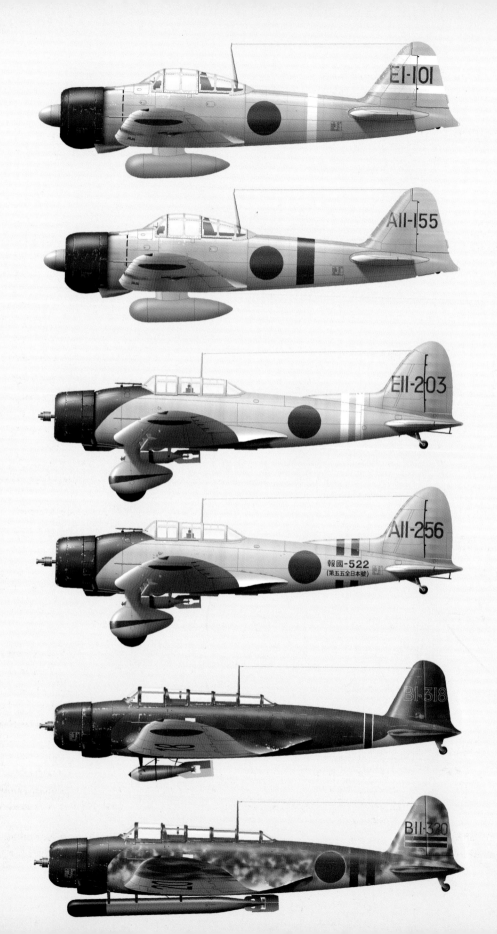

## Organization of Pearl Harbor Attack Force

### First Attack Force (First Wave) (Commander Fuchida Mitsuo)

| | | Carrier | Aircraft Type | Number | Target |
|---|---|---|---|---|---|
| First Flight – Horizontal Bombing Force (Commander Fuchida Mitsuo) | 1st Attack Unit | *Akagi* | B5N Type 97 | 15 | Battleship Row |
| | 2nd Attack Unit | *Kaga* | B5N Type 97 | 15 (1 abort) | Battleship Row |
| | 3rd Attack Group | *Soryu* | B5N Type 97 | 10 | Battleship Row |
| | 4th Attack Group | *Hiryu* | B5N Type 97 | 10 | Battleship Row |
| | All aircraft armed with a single Type 5 800kg bomb | | | **Total: 50 (49 actually attacked)** | |
| First Flight Special Group – Torpedo Force (Lieutenant Commander Murata Shigeharu) | 1st Torpedo Attack Unit | *Akagi* | B5N Type 97 | 12 | Battleship Row |
| | 2nd Torpedo Attack Unit | *Kaga* | B5N Type 97 | 12 | Battleship Row |
| | 3rd Torpedo Attack Unit | *Soryu* | B5N Type 97 | 8 | Carriers, Battleships |
| | 4th Torpedo Attack Unit | *Hiryu* | B5N Type 97 | 8 | Carriers, Battleships |
| | All aircraft armed with a single Type 91 air-launched torpedo | | | **Total: 40** | |
| Second Flight – Dive Bomber Force (Lieutenant Commander Takahashi Kakuichi) | 15th Attack Unit | *Shokaku* | D3A Type 99 | 27 (1 abort) | 9 against Ford Island, 17 against Hickam Fld. |
| | 16th Attack Unit | *Zuikaku* | D3A Type 99 | 27 (2 abort) | Wheeler Field |
| | All aircraft armed with a single 250kg general-purpose bomb | | | **Total: 54 (51 actually attacked)** | |
| Third Flight – Air Control Force (Lieutenant Commander Itaya Shigeru) | 1st Fighter Combat Unit | *Akagi* | A6M Type 00 | 9 | Ford Island/Hickam Fld. |
| | 2nd Fighter Combat Unit | *Kaga* | A6M Type 00 | 9 | Ford Island/Hickam Fld. |
| | 3rd Fighter Combat Unit | *Soryu* | A6M Type 00 | 9 (1 abort) | Wheeler Fld./Ewa |
| | 4th Fighter Combat Unit | *Hiryu* | A6M Type 00 | 6 | Wheeler Fld./Ewa |
| | 5th Fighter Combat Unit | *Shokaku* | A6M Type 00 | 6 (1 abort) | Kaneohe |
| | 6th Fighter Combat Unit | *Zuikaku* | A6M Type 00 | 6 | Kaneohe |
| | All aircraft armed with two 20mm cannon and two 7.7mm machine guns | | | **Total: 45 (43 actually attacked)** | |
| **Total aircraft in first wave** | | | | **189 (183 actually attacked)** | |

### Second Attack Force (Second Wave) (Lieutenant Commander Shimazaki Shigekazu)

| | | Carrier | Aircraft Type | Number | Target |
|---|---|---|---|---|---|
| First Flight – Horizontal Bombing Force (Lieutenant Commander Shimazaki Shigekazu) | 5th Attack Unit | *Shokaku* | B5N Type 97 | 27 | 9 against Ford Island 18 against Kaneohe |
| | 6th Attack Unit | *Zuikaku* | B5N Type 97 | 27 | Hickam Field |
| | Half armed with two 250kg bombs; half armed with one 250kg bomb and six 60kg bombs | | | **Total: 54** | |
| Second Flight – Dive Bomber Force (Lieutenant Commander Egusa Takashige) | 11th Attack Unit | *Akagi* | D3A Type 99 | 18 | Various naval targets |
| | 12th Attack Unit | *Kaga* | D3A Type 99 | 27 (1 abort) | Various naval targets |
| | 13th Attack Unit | *Soryu* | D3A Type 99 | 18 (1 abort) | Various naval targets |
| | 14th Attack Unit | *Hiryu* | D3A Type 99 | 18 (1 abort) | Various naval targets |
| | All aircraft armed with a single 250kg bomb | | | **Total: 81 (78 actually attacked)** | |
| Third Flight – Air Control Force (Lieutenant Shindo Saburo) | 1st Fighter Combat Unit | *Akagi* | A6M Type 00 | 9 | Ford Island/Hickam Fld. |
| | 2nd Fighter Combat Unit | *Kaga* | A6M Type 00 | 9 | Ford Island/Hickam Fld. |
| | 3rd Fighter Combat Unit | *Soryu* | A6M Type 00 | 9 | Kaneohe |
| | 4th Fighter Combat Unit | *Hiryu* | A6M Type 00 | 9 (1 abort) | Kaneohe/Bellows Field |
| | All aircraft armed with two 20mm cannon and two 7.7mm machine guns | | | **Total: 36 (35 actually attacked)** | |
| **Total aircraft in second wave** | | | | **171 (167 actually attacked)** | |
| **Total attacking aircraft** | | | | **360 (350 actually attacked)** | |

spotted on the flight deck and launched. This was the method selected for the Pearl Harbor attack. Two waves were planned, with each of the six carriers launching about half its fighters in the first wave to escort one of the ship's attack squadrons. The second wave was organized in a similar manner, but utilized the other attack squadron.

The target priorities of the attack were laid out in Annex 3 of Operation Order Number 1. This order, issued on November 1 from the Combined Fleet to the First Carrier Striking Force, stated, "Targets for attack are airfields; aircraft carriers; battleships, cruisers and other warships; merchant shipping; port facilities and land installations, in that order."

The table on page 25 shows how Nagumo and his staff operationalized this directive. The elite carrier attack planes of the First and Second Carrier Divisions were earmarked to destroy ships moored around Ford Island by a combination of 40 torpedo and 50 horizontal bombers. The inexperienced pilots of the recently operational Fifth Carrier Division were not trusted to attack ships, but the 54 aircraft were instead earmarked to attack bases at Ford Island, Hickam Field, and Kaneohe to cripple American air power. The 45 fighters were tasked to strafe Hickam and Kaneohe.

The time of the attack was altered late in the planning process. To accommodate the relatively unskilled airmen of the Fifth Carrier Division, which could not conduct night flying, the time of the attack was moved from dawn to 0800hrs. This required a launch at 0600hrs just as dawn was breaking, and still put the raiders over the target in daylight and early enough to gain surprise.

## The Attack Plan in Detail

The first wave would launch at 0600hrs 230 miles north of Oahu, and include 189 aircraft. The attack would begin at 0800hrs Hawaii time, catching the Americans at their most vulnerable. The key to the first wave, and the entire operation, was the 40 torpedo bombers under command of Murata and the 50 level bombers under Fuchida. These were targeted on the battleships and carriers around Ford Island. The 54 dive-bombers under Takahashi were ordered to attack air installations at Ford Island, Wheeler, and Hickam Fields to cripple any American air response. The fighters were charged with gaining air control and then attacking the various air installations.

This vertical photograph taken on November 10, 1941 gives a close-up of Ford Island and the mooring points around it. In the upper left is Battleship Row with five battleships present. At the bottom of the image are carrier *Lexington*, a seaplane tender, and a light cruiser. As shown here, carriers often moored on Ford Island's northwestern side and the Japanese had given these targets top priority. The Naval Air Station at Ford Island was the home of two squadrons of patrol aircraft and hosted carrier aircraft when their parent ship was in port. Approximately 21 PBY patrol planes are parked at the Naval Air Station's seaplane base seen in the upper right. (Naval History and Heritage Command)

Two variant plans for the first wave were developed. The first assumed surprise. In this case, the vulnerable torpedo planes would sweep in first to take full advantage of surprise while the other strike aircraft circled north of the harbor. If surprise was not gained, then the dive-bombers would strike first, followed by the level bombers. In the confusion and chaos, the torpedo planes would enter the fray last.

Fuchida instructed each of the level-bomber groups to carefully assess their situation before releasing their bombs. The level bombers would approach against the wind to improve accuracy and each group was ordered to make as many passes as necessary to ensure an accurate drop. The pilots were instructed to mass their fire against a few targets in order to ensure their destruction; minor damage against a number of targets was considered failure. The level bombers were ordered to focus on the battleships moored in pairs as this presented a larger target.

The 40 torpedo planes were to attack in two groups, ideally at the same instant. Murata would lead the main section of 24 aircraft, which were to fly to a point south of the harbor entrance, then swing north over Hickam Field and attack Battleship Row. The remaining 16 would attack from the

The second attack wave from *Shokaku* prepares to launch. The identity of the ship is confirmed by the markings of the aircraft. Aircraft from the Fifth Carrier Division were assigned secondary targets during both attack waves. (Naval History and Heritage Command)

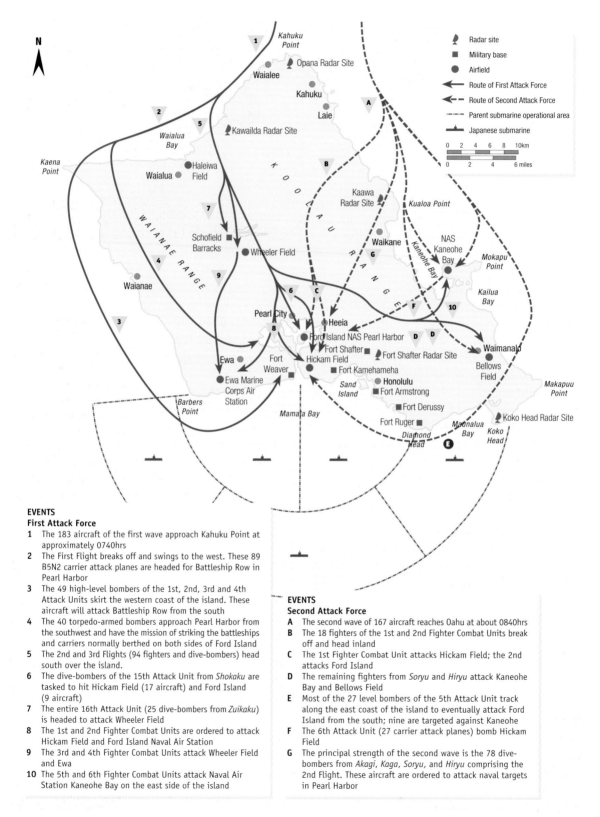

## EVENTS
### First Attack Force

1 The 183 aircraft of the first wave approach Kahuku Point at approximately 0740hrs

2 The First Flight breaks off and swings to the west. These 89 B5N2 carrier attack planes are headed for Battleship Row in Pearl Harbor

3 The 49 high-level bombers of the 1st, 2nd, 3rd and 4th Attack Units skirt the western coast of the island. These aircraft will attack Battleship Row from the south

4 The 40 torpedo-armed bombers approach Pearl Harbor from the southwest and have the mission of striking the battleships and carriers normally berthed on both sides of Ford Island

5 The 2nd and 3rd Flights (94 fighters and dive-bombers) head south over the island.

6 The dive-bombers of the 15th Attack Unit from *Shokaku* are tasked to hit Hickam Field (17 aircraft) and Ford Island (9 aircraft)

7 The entire 16th Attack Unit (25 dive-bombers from *Zuikaku*) is headed to attack Wheeler Field

8 The 1st and 2nd Fighter Combat Units are ordered to attack Hickam Field and Ford Island Naval Air Station

9 The 3rd and 4th Fighter Combat Units attack Wheeler Field and Ewa

10 The 5th and 6th Fighter Combat Units attack Naval Air Station Kaneohe Bay on the east side of the island

### EVENTS
### Second Attack Force

A The second wave of 167 aircraft reaches Oahu at about 0840hrs

B The 18 fighters of the 1st and 2nd Fighter Combat Units break off and head inland

C The 1st Fighter Combat Unit attacks Hickam Field; the 2nd attacks Ford Island

D The remaining fighters from *Soryu* and *Hiryu* attack Kaneohe Bay and Bellows Field

E Most of the 27 level bombers of the 5th Attack Unit track along the east coast of the island to eventually attack Ford Island from the south; nine are targeted against Kaneohe

F The 6th Attack Unit (27 carrier attack planes) bomb Hickam Field

G The principal strength of the second wave is the 78 dive-bombers from *Akagi*, *Kaga*, *Soryu*, and *Hiryu* comprising the 2nd Flight. These aircraft are ordered to attack naval targets in Pearl Harbor

The Japanese Attack Plan

west and northwest against the targets moored on that side of Ford Island. The Japanese feared that the Americans had placed torpedo nets around the battleships, which had a potential to derail the entire attack, but Genda and Fuchida had prepared in case they were encountered. Realizing the importance of destroying such a defense and the unlikelihood of destroying the nets with torpedoes, Fuchida and Genda had made arrangements with the torpedo plane pilots to crash their planes directly on to them to open the way for succeeding aircraft.

The second wave would arrive shortly after the first, allowing the defenders no time for recovery. This strike was very different. No torpedo planes were included because, with the element of surprise lost, the low and slow profiles of the torpedo bombers would have resulted in heavy losses. There were 54 level bombers under Shimazaki's personal command; he also acted as the overall leader of the second wave. These were targeted on Hickam, Kaneohe, and Ford Island to complete the destruction of American air power. The real punch of the second wave was the 81 dive-bombers under Egusa; these were slated to attack naval targets. Of particular emphasis were any carriers damaged from the first wave. The dive-bombers would attack them again and complete their destruction in hopes of making any salvage impossible.

Pre-attack scouting was a key in the mind of Genda. It was vital to get last-second information on the location of the American fleet so that Fuchida could deploy his forces accordingly. The intent was to launch a single floatplane from cruisers *Tone* and *Chikuma* to scout Pearl Harbor and the fleet anchorage at Lahaina. Initially it was planned to launch the search planes one hour before the main launch. However, it was feared that these aircraft would be discovered and that one hour gave the defenders too much potential time to prepare. Genda and Nagumo cut the time to only 30 minutes to retain surprise. Radio silence was key; only Fuchida would open communications. If surprise was gained he would give the appropriate signal to his attack units and then signal, "*Tora! Tora! Tora!*" (Tiger! Tiger! Tiger!) back to Nagumo's flagship.

Final planning was not completed until the end of October and it continued to be tweaked even after the task force left Japan. On November 2 the outline of the plan and the role for each participating unit was revealed in a mass briefing aboard flagship *Akagi* in Ariake Bay. Following two more weeks of exercise, the fleet re-supplied and then departed their homeports in ones or twos to rendezvous in Hitokappu Bay in the Kuriles on November 22. One final briefing was held aboard *Akagi* on November 23 during which every unit in the fleet was informed of the objective. Two days later the fleet departed to change history.

A Type 0 carrier fighter takes off from *Akagi*. The fighter is identified by its tail code (AI-108) and the single red band around the fuselage. Japanese fighters were successful in causing heavy losses to American aircraft on the ground by strafing, but were not as successful in air-to-air engagements against the few American fighters that were able to get airborne during the raid. (Naval History and Heritage Command)

**DECEMBER 7 1941**

**0755hrs Ford Island Naval Air Station and Hickam Field attacked; torpedo bombers attack ships moored on northwest side of Ford Island**

Fleet submarine *I-8* shown in a 1939 photo. This J3 type was the largest Japanese submarine built before the war. It was employed in the Pearl Harbor operation as a squadron flagship. On December 17, *I-8* used its embarked floatplane to perform a reconnaissance of Pearl Harbor to confirm damage results. The Imperial Navy's submarine force was an integral part of the Hawaii operation, but proved totally unsuccessful. (Yamato Museum)

## The Submarine Plan

A largely forgotten aspect of the Hawaii operation was the massive commitment of 30 Imperial Navy fleet submarines in support of the attack. The Japanese had devoted considerable resources to developing a submarine force capable of operations at extended range as part of their attrition strategy against the US Navy, and their submarines were manned by well-equipped crews and provided with reliable torpedoes. Several different types of submarines were available, including cruiser submarines, command submarines, and a number of boats equipped with floatplanes for scout duties. Much was expected of the submarine force, and many Japanese admirals anticipated that the overall damage inflicted by the submarines over an extended period would exceed any damage caused by the air attack. The commitment of the submarine force was viewed as an insurance against failure by the untested aircraft carriers.

The Sixth Fleet, the Imperial Navy's submarine force, was informed by Yamamoto on July 29 that it would play a role in the Pearl Harbor operation. It speaks to the confidence Yamamoto had in his submarine force, but also to the uncertainty over the effectiveness of carrier air power, which was still untested. With the entire Hawaii operation seen as a giant risk, there was little harm in adding the submarines into the equation. In late October it was decided to add another dimension into the attack – five of the fleet submarines were to carry midget submarines to Oahu and these were ordered to penetrate Pearl Harbor.

The submarines were ordered to transit to the Hawaiian Islands by moving only at night on the surface and at much slower submerged speeds during the day. Nevertheless, the movement of such a large force over such a large distance carried with it a great potential for discovery; such a discovery might jeopardize the entire operation. The potential for discovery was greatly enhanced when the five submarines designated to carry the midget submarines closed on Oahu, and when the midget submarines themselves transited into the harbor.

It was Yamamoto who authorized the inclusion of the midget submarines, against the advice of Genda and other Combined Fleet staff officers. In response to the emotional pleas of the crews, Yamamoto further approved that they could proceed inside Pearl Harbor even before the arrival of the air raid. It is hard to reconcile why Yamamoto put the honor of ten submarine crewmen above the risk that their activities could jeopardize the whole operation.

The 30 submarines committed to the Hawaii operation were divided into five groups. Three submarines (*I-19*, *I-21*, and *I-23*) were actually part of the

First Carrier Striking Force and were to act as reconnaissance units in advance of the carrier force on its path across the North Pacific. During the attack these same units would be available to rescue downed aircrew and help defend the carrier force from counterattack. Another four submarines (I-9, I-15, I-17, and I-25) formed the First Submarine Group and were positioned to form a picket line 150 miles north of Oahu. These were assigned the mission of attacking units fleeing from the air attack or advancing in the direction of the carrier force.

Another seven submarines (I-1, I-2, I-3, I-4, I-5, I-6, and I-7) comprised the Second Submarine Group. These units were deployed in a picket line from Oahu to Molokai, guarding the Kaili Channel. Nine submarines comprised the Third Submarine Group – I-8, I-68, I-69, I-70, I-71, I-72, I-73, I-74, and I-75. This force was deployed in a line south of Oahu. Two of the submarines were ordered to scout the Lahaina anchorage, where the Japanese suspected the Pacific Fleet could be located if it was not in Pearl Harbor. If the fleet was located in the anchorage, submarines would guard the three channels leading into the anchorage and other submarines would be moved off their stations near Pearl Harbor against the anchorage. I-74 was assigned the duty of acting as an aircrew rescue unit by lying off Niihau Island, which had been designated as an emergency landing area for those aircraft too damaged to proceed back to their carrier. Two additional submarines loosely supported the Hawaii operation. I-10 scouted Suva Island on November 29 and Pago Pago Island on December 4; I-26 scouted four locations in the Aleutian Islands from November 25 to 30.

The final five submarines comprised the Special Attack Group. Submarines I-16, I-18, I-20, I-22, and I-24 were modified to carry a midget submarine each. The original plan was that the five submarines would reach a position some 300 nautical miles south of Oahu by December 3 and then spend the next several days slowly closing on the island in order not to be discovered. The midget submarines would then be launched after the air attack to deal with American warships fleeing the harbor. However, after the protests of the crews it was decided that the midget submarines would be allowed to enter Pearl Harbor and attack during the air raid. This obviously meant that the slow submarines would have to move inside the harbor before the attack had begun, thus greatly increasing the potential for discovery.

The results of the midget submarine attack will be described later. The results of the fleet submarines can be described succinctly as a total failure. In spite of the hundreds of ships going in and out of Pearl Harbor on December 7 and days following, not a single one was even attacked by Japanese submarines, much less sunk. On December 10 submarines did spot an American carrier (Enterprise) east of Oahu and several submarines were dispatched to engage this lucrative target. The carrier was not attacked, and one submarine was sunk by American air attack. The total bag in the days following the attack was a paltry three merchant ships. This was the start of a generally unsuccessful war for the Imperial Navy's submarine force.

# THE RAID

## The Approach

At 0600hrs on November 26 the First Carrier Striking Force departed its anchorage at Hitokappu Bay. From there, its transit to the planned attack launch point 230 miles north of Oahu required 13 days. The slow transit was dominated by the need for constant refueling, with the destroyers having to refuel every other day. To make the transit, carriers *Akagi*, *Hiryu*, and *Soryu* were forced to carry fuel in converted voids and in drums stored throughout the ships. *Akagi* carried an extra 1,400 tons of fuel in this manner.

Even in the desolate North Pacific Ocean, there was the constant fear of discovery. To test the security of the planned transit route, the passenger liner *Taiyo Maru* departed Japan on October 22 en route to Honolulu, where it arrived November 1. It reported that no ships were encountered and that the sea conditions would allow for refueling operations. During its transit through the rough waters of the North Pacific Ocean, the First Carrier Striking Force encountered no ships. Up until December 2, there was the possibility that diplomatic efforts would succeed and that the strike force

*Kaga* steams through heavy North Pacific seas en route to attack Pearl Harbor. The picture is taken from *Akagi*; *Zuikaku* is at right. (Naval History and Heritage Command)

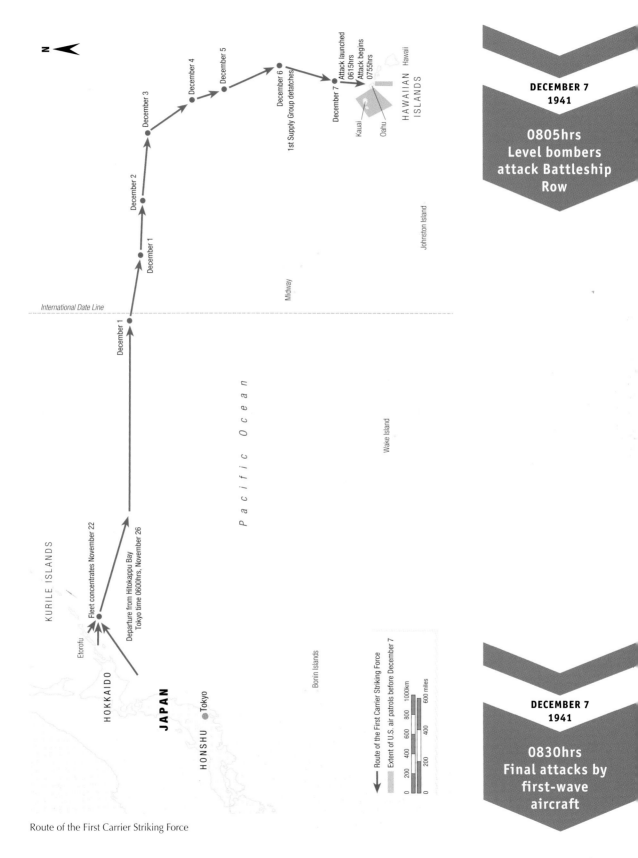

Route of the First Carrier Striking Force

**DECEMBER 7 1941**

**0805hrs Level bombers attack Battleship Row**

**DECEMBER 7 1941**

**0830hrs Final attacks by first-wave aircraft**

would be recalled. This was put to rest when the following message was received at 2000hrs: "Climb Mount Niitaka 1208". This meant that the attack would begin as scheduled on December 8, Japanese time.

Tensions mounted as the attack force grew nearer to its target. The Japanese believed that American air reconnaissance from Oahu was poor toward the north. In fact, the Americans were only flying patrols to the west and south, so there was no chance of the Japanese being discovered as they approached from the north. The Second Supply Group departed the formation around noon on December 5; the First Supply Group departed around 0800hrs on December 6. With every ship in the force topped off with fuel, speed was increased and at 1130hrs the strike force changed course to 180 degrees – straight for Hawaii. Minutes later, the famous Z flag was raised on *Akagi* – the same flag hoisted by Admiral Togo before the famous Japanese victory at the battle of Tsushima.

Last-minute intelligence generated by the Japanese consulate in Honolulu and received aboard *Akagi* suggested that conditions for the attack were favorable. At 0150hrs on December 7 a message was received; it informed that as of December 6 nine battleships, three light cruisers, three seaplane tenders, and 17 destroyers were present in harbor. An additional four light cruisers and two destroyers were in docks. Unfortunately for the Japanese, the report indicated that all heavy cruisers and the carriers were absent. The report was not entirely accurate, but the bulk of the Pacific Fleet appeared to be present. A few minutes later a report was received which indicated that no barrage balloons or torpedo nets were in evidence.

### First Carrier Striking Force (Hawaii Operation)

| | |
|---|---|
| Aircraft carriers | *Akagi* (flag), *Kaga, Soryu, Hiryu, Shokaku, Zuikaku* |
| Battleships | *Hiei, Kirishima* |
| Heavy Cruisers | *Tone, Chikuma* |
| Light Cruiser | *Abukuma* |
| Destroyers | *Akigumo, Hamakaze, Isokaze, Kagero, Shiranuhi, Tanikaze, Urakaze* |
| Submarines | *I-19, I-21, I-23* |
| First Supply Group | Four tankers escorted by destroyer *Kasumi* |
| Second Supply Group | Three tankers escorted by destroyer *Arare* |

## The Battle Opens

The first shot in the war between Japan and the United States was fired not as a result of the air raid on Pearl Harbor but as a result of the movement of the midget submarines into the harbor. Just as Fuchida and the airmen of the First Carrier Striking Force had feared, these submarines jeopardized the surprise of the entire operation. The first shot was fired by the destroyer *Ward* at 0645hrs when the World War I veteran destroyer sighted the sail of one of Yamamoto's five midget submarines making its way into the channel leading to the harbor. The submarine had been sighted as early as 0342hrs earlier that morning by minesweeper *Condor* patrolling south of the submarine gate leading into the channel. *Ward* regained contact at 0637hrs and shortly thereafter made a gun attack followed by a depth-charge attack. This action resulted in a report to fleet command at about 0720hrs. Though the fleet commander was summoned, there was no attempt to alert ships in the harbor and no attempt to inform the Army that an act of war had already been committed.

The US Army was charged with the defense of the installations and ships on Oahu from enemy attack. Lieutenant General Walter C. Short was in command of the Hawaiian Department with overall responsibility for the islands' defense, and Major General Frederick L. Martin was in command of the Hawaiian Air Force. Together, they controlled six radar stations, over 200 aircraft, and an extensive array of antiaircraft guns – surely adequate to perform the mission of defending the fleet from air attack. However, the Americans' defensive effort was undermined by a critical underestimation of the capabilities of the Japanese. Nobody on Hawaii or even in Washington believed that the Japanese had the capability to open a war against the United States by striking Hawaii. This fatal misapprehension more than anything else explains the general lack of battle readiness present on the island on December 7.

Further handicapping Short was a general lack of cooperation between the army and the navy. Even Short and Martin saws things differently. Short, an infantry officer, was obsessed with the notion that sabotage was the greatest threat to his aircraft. Accordingly, he ordered that all aircraft be lined up close together on their home fields to facilitate guarding them against sabotage. Martin was caught in the middle when all his commanders demanded that the aircraft be dispersed.

Though there was confusion caused by an organization where Short controlled the antiaircraft guns and the radars while Martin controlled the aircraft and the Air Information Center, there was reason to believe that the assets in place were inadequate to perform their mission. Two major exercises had been held with the navy in 1941. In one of these, on November 12, a navy carrier launched a strike from 80 miles off Oahu. Army radar picked up the attackers, identified them, and had fighters up within six minutes to intercept the attacking force 30 miles from the island. This exercise was heavily scripted but it showed what could be done with operational radar units, a fully staffed Air Information Center, and armed and ready aircraft. On December 7, none of these elements were fully in place.

During the week before December 7, the entire Hawaiian Department was engaged in a full exercise that Short judged as a great success. The exercise was terminated on December 6, a Saturday, and after their equipment had been properly returned and secured, personnel were told to report back for duty that next Monday. Thus, on December 7 the radar stations were manned for only three hours in the morning, there were no experienced personnel on watch at the Air Information Center, and of the 75 operational P-40 and P-36 fighters, none were fully armed and ready.

In spite of the general lack of readiness, the army gathered ample evidence of the imminent attack on the morning of December 7. There were five operational SC-270 radar sites on the island (a sixth radar was on the island but had not yet been deployed). Lacking spare parts and

**Pearl Harbor ship locations, 0755hrs, December 7, 1941**

**KEY**

No. = ship's number
c. = date commissioned
conv. = date converted
BB = battleship
DD = destroyer
CA = heavy cruiser
CL = light cruiser
SS = submarine
CM = minelayer
DM = light minelayer
DMS = fast minesweeper
YMS = minesweeper
PT = motor torpedo boats
AD = destroyer tender
AV = seaplane tender
AH = hospital ship
AK = cargo ship
AO = oil tanker
AR = repair ship
AX = auxiliary ship
PG = patrol gunboat

1. Phoenix (Brooklyn class, No.46: CL, c.1938)
2. Blue (Craven class, No.387: DD, c.1937)
3. Whitney (AD, No.4: c.1919)
4. Conyngham (Mahan class, No.371: DD, c.1936)
5. Reid (Mahan class, No.369: DD, c.1937)
6. Tucker (Mahan class, No.374: DD, c.1936)
7. Case (Mahan class, No.370: DD, c.1935)
8. Selfridge (Porter class, No.357: DD, c.1937)
9. Ralph Talbot (Craven class, No.390: DD, c.1938)
10. Patterson (Craven class, No.392: DD, c.1938)
11. Henley (Craven class, No.391: DD, c.1937)
12. Aylwin (Farragut class, No.355: DD, c.1935)
13. Farragut (DD, No.348: c.1934)
14. Dale (Farragut class, No.353: DD, c.1935)
15. Monaghan (Farragut class, No.354: DD, c.1933)
16. Ramsay (DM, No.16: conv.1930)
17. Gamble (DM, No.15: conv.1931)
18. Montgomery (DM, No.17: conv.1931)
19. Trever (DMS, No.16: conv.1940)
20. Breese (DM, No.18: conv.1931)
21. Zane (DMS, No.14: conv.1940)
22. Perry (DMS, No.17: conv.1940)
23. Wasmuth (DMS, No.15: conv.1940)
24. Medusa (AR, No.1: c.1924)
25. Curtiss (AV, No.4: c.1940)
26. Tangier (AV, No.8: c.1940)
27. Utah (Ex-BB, No.31: c.1911)
28. Raleigh (Omaha class, No.7: CL, c.1922)
29. Detroit (Omaha class, No.8: CL, c.1922)

30. Phelps (Porter class, No.360: DD, c.1936)
31. MacDonough (Farragut class, No.351: DD, c.1935)
32. Worden (Farragut class, No.352: DD, c.1934)
33. Dewey (Farragut class, No.349: DD, c.1934)
34. Hull (Farragut class, No.350: DD, c.1935)
35. Dobbin (AD, No.3: c.1924)
36. Solace (AH, No.5: c.1941)
37. Allen (DD, No.66: c.1916)
38. Chew (DD, No.106: c.1918)
39. Nevada (Oklahoma class, No.36: BB, c.1914)
40. Vestal (AR, No.4: c.1909)
41. Arizona (Pennsylvania class, No.39: BB, c.1916)
42. Tennessee (California class, No.43: BB, c.1919)
43. West Virginia (Maryland class, No.48: BB, c.1921)
44. Maryland (BB, No.46: c.1920)
45. Oklahoma (BB, No.37: c.1914)
46. Neosho (No.23: AO)
47. California (BB, No.44: c.1919)
48. Avocet (AV, c.1918)
49. Helm (Craven class, No.388: DD, c.1937)
50. Bobolink (YMS, No.20: c.1919)
51. Vireo (YMS, No.52: c.1919)
52. Rail (YMS, No.26: c.1918)
53. Tern (YMS, No.31: c.1919)
54. Shaw (Mahan class, No.373: DD, c.1935)
55. Cassin (Mahan class, No.372: DD, c.1933)
56. Downes (Mahan class, No.375: DD, c.1933)
57. Pennsylvania (BB, No.38: c.1915)
58. Oglala (CM, No.4: c.1917)

59. Cachalot (SS, No.170: c.1933)
60. Helena (St. Louis class, No.50: CL, c.1938)
61. Jarvis (Craven class, No.393: DD, c.1934)
62. Argonne (AX, No.31: c.1921)
63. Sacramento (PG, No.19: c.1914)
64. Mugford (Craven class, No.389: DD, c.1934)
65. Rigel (AD, No.13: c.1921)
66. Cummings (Mahan class, No.365: DD, c.1937)
67. Honolulu (Brooklyn class, No.48: CL, c.1937)
68. Schley (No.103: DD, c.1918)
69. Ramapo (No.12: AO)
70. San Francisco (Astoria class, No.38: CA, c.1934)
71. New Orleans (Astoria class, No.32: CA, c.1932)
72. Preble (DM, No.20: conv.1937)
73. Swan (AV, No.7: c.1919)
74. St. Louis (CL, No.49: c.1938)
75. Bagley (Craven class, No.386: DD, c.1938)
76. Tracy (DM, No.19: conv.1937)
77. Pruitt (DM, No.22: conv.1937)
78. Grebe (YMS, No.43: c.1919)
79. Sicard (DM, No.21: conv.1937)
80. Thornton (AV, No.11: conv.1939)
81. Hulbert (AV, No.6: conv.1939)
82. Tautog (SS, No.199: T class, c.1940)
83. Dolphin (SS, No.169: D type, c.1932)
84. Narwhal (SS No.167: N type, c.1930)
85. Pelias (SS tender, No.14: c.1941)
86. Sumner (AX, No.32: c.1913)
87. Castor (AK, No.1: c.1940)

trained operators, these sites were scheduled to operate from only 0400–0700hrs. The first unknown contact gained by these radars that morning was at 0613hrs when the Koko Head and Fort Shafter radars picked up and tracked single contacts south of Oahu. At 0645hrs the radars at Kaawa, Opana, and Kawailoa detected a group of aircraft north of the island. All except the Opana radar shut down as scheduled at 0700hrs. Just as the Opana radar was due to be shut down, the two-man crew picked up a large flight of aircraft 132 miles north of Oahu. This information was reported at 0702hrs to the Air Information Center at Fort Shafter. On watch at the time were only two personnel, with a lieutenant in charge standing only his second watch. After talking to one of the operators, the lieutenant decided that the incoming formation was a flight of B-17s which was due that morning from the United States. This was at 0720hrs. The Opana radar continued to track the inbound flight until 0739hrs when it was only 20 miles away.

The condition of the US Pacific Fleet under Admiral Husband E. Kimmel was similarly unready for battle. Kimmel had agreed with Short that the navy would assume the responsibility of long-range patrol from the Hawaiian Air Force, which lacked adequate numbers of aircraft to perform this mission. Though Kimmel had an adequate number of long-range patrol aircraft on the island to perform a full 360-degree search, he decided that it was wiser to maintain the overall readiness of his force to support the movement of the fleet once war began, rather than to wear them down in constant patrol duties. This meant that only a cursory search to the south and west of Oahu was performed, leaving the north unwatched.

Nevertheless, in one very important respect, the Pacific Fleet was fortunate. On the morning of December 7, there were a total of 82 warships at Pearl Harbor. However, none of the fleet's three carriers were present. *Enterprise* was at sea with three cruisers and nine destroyers delivering aircraft to Wake Island. *Lexington* had departed Pearl Harbor on December 5 with three cruisers and five destroyers on a ferry mission to Midway. The fleet's third carrier, *Saratoga*, was at Puget Sound on the West Coast undergoing repairs. Of the nine battleships assigned to the Pacific Fleet, eight were in Pearl Harbor. Of these, seven were arrayed in "Battleship Row" moored around Ford Island and another was in dry dock in the navy yard. The ninth battleship, *Colorado*, was also at Puget Sound. There were also two heavy cruisers, six light, 30 destroyers and five submarines present at Pearl Harbor.

## The Attack Inbound

At 0530hrs, the heavy cruisers *Tone* and *Chikuma* each launched a seaplane. *Chikuma*'s aircraft was assigned to scout Pearl Harbor while *Tone*'s aircraft was ordered to scout the Lahaina anchorage and search south of Oahu for American carriers. The search planes were not to overfly their targets, but to observe from a distance. Fuchida thought that it was so important to get last-minute

**DECEMBER 7 1941**

**0836hrs Midget submarine spotted by several ships inside harbor**

The commanding officer of *Shokaku* watches as planes take off to attack Pearl Harbor. The kanji inscription at left is an exhortation for the ship's pilots to do their duty. *Shokaku* lost no planes in the attack. (Naval History and Heritage Command)

A Type 97 carrier attack plane takes off from either *Zuikaku* or *Shokaku* as the second-wave attack is launched. The aircrew is being exhorted on by cheering ship's crewmen. (Naval History and Heritage Command)

intelligence on the Pacific Fleet that he took the risk of the aircraft being detected by radar and allowed them to break radio silence to make their reports.

By 0530hrs the first wave had been spotted on the flight decks of the six carriers and the engines of the aircraft started to warm up. The aircraft were manned at 0550hrs. The fleet headed east to turn into the wind in order to get sufficient wind across the deck for launch, and increased speed to 24 knots. The weather on this morning was some of the worst yet encountered on the transit.

At 0615hrs, the first wave began taking off. The entire group was in the air in 15 minutes. One fighter crashed on take-off and another aborted due to engine problems. Three dive-bombers and a carrier attack aircraft armed as a horizontal bomber also aborted. After taking off and circling near their carriers, the entire strike force assembled into a single loose formation and headed south while gradually assuming its cruising altitude. The formation of 183 aircraft was led by the 89 carrier attack aircraft from *Akagi*, *Kaga*, *Soryu* and *Hiryu* flying at between 9,200 and 9,800ft. To their right were the 51 dive-bombers from *Shokaku* and *Zuikaku* flying at 14,100ft. The fighter cover was provided by the Type 00 fighters from all six carriers, which were positioned above the formation at 14,100ft.

As soon as the first wave was launched, preparations began for launching the second. These aircraft were quickly spotted on the flight decks and their engines warmed. At 0705hrs the fleet again turned into the wind to begin a second launch; this began at 0715hrs and also went quickly and efficiently. One aircraft, a *Hiryu* dive-bomber, had engine problems and did not launch, and after launch, two more dive-bombers and a fighter had to return due to engine problems. This put a total of 167 aircraft in the second wave, which now headed south to Oahu.

Type 99 carrier bombers, probably from the second wave, prepare to launch. The ship in the background is *Soryu*. (Naval History and Heritage Command)

At 0735hrs, the airborne strike received word from *Chikuma*'s search plane that nine battleships, one heavy and six light cruisers were present in harbor. A subsequent report indicated that weather conditions were perfect. Earlier, *Tone*'s scout plane had reported that Lahaina anchorage was clear.

## The First Attack Force

At 0740hrs, just as the formation was approaching land off Kahuku Point, attack leader Fuchida fired one flare from his carrier attack plane. This was the signal that surprise had been achieved and it meant that the attack would open with the more vulnerable torpedo bombers executing their attack runs first. However, fearing that the fighters flying above had not seen his first signal, Fuchida fired another flare. Though the two flares were far enough apart not to be taken as the same signal, the result was confusion as two flares were the sign that surprise had not been achieved. The dive-bombers and fighters mistakenly rushed ahead to lead the attack in order to draw fire from the vulnerable torpedo planes.

Minutes later, at 0749hrs, Fuchida issued the attack signal. The formation now began to divide as the different groups of aircraft headed for their respective targets. At 0753hrs Fuchida's aircraft sent the signal "*Tora! Tora! Tora!*" indicating that surprise had been gained. This signal was picked up not only by the First Carrier Striking Force, but also aboard Yamamoto's flagship *Nagato* located in the Inland Sea.

## The Torpedo Attack

Though it was not first as Fuchida had intended, the attack by the 40 carrier attack planes armed as torpedo bombers was the most important component of the Japanese plan. The target of these aircraft was the American battleships anchored around Ford Island. Of the eight battleships present, five were potentially vulnerable to torpedo attack. The torpedo bombers were led by Lieutenant Commander Murata Shigeharu from the *Akagi* air group. At 0751hrs he ordered his formation to split up into four groups, each built around the torpedo bombers from one of the four carriers contributing aircraft. Twenty-four of the aircraft under Murata's command, 12 each from *Akagi* and *Kaga*, flew to the southeast in order to loop around Hickam Field to enable a direct approach to the ships on Battleship Row located on the eastern side of Ford Island. The remaining 16 torpedo bombers (eight each from *Soryu* and *Hiryu*) flew to the east so as to attack the ships anchored on the western side of Ford Island. The carriers that were often moored here were the top priority of the torpedo attack, and Genda had allocated 16 torpedoes to the two carriers which could be present. Pre-attack intelligence had

This view was taken from a Japanese aircraft and shows the early stages of the attack. Ford Island is in the foreground, and in the distance are the Navy Yard and the Submarine Base. A torpedo has just hit *West Virginia* on the far side of Ford Island. The other outboard battleship is *Oklahoma*, which has already been torpedoed and is listing to port. On the near side of Ford Island, to the left, are light cruisers *Detroit* and *Raleigh*, training ship *Utah* and seaplane tender *Tangier*. *Raleigh* and *Utah* have been torpedoed, and *Utah* is listing sharply to port. Two Japanese torpedo planes can be seen banking away after launching their weapons. (Naval History and Heritage Command)

# FIRST ATTACK WAVE AGAINST TARGETS IN PEARL HARBOR

**0750–0811HRS, DECEMBER 7, 1941**

PEARL CITY

FORD ISLAND

WAIPIO PENINSULA

## US FORCES   1 – 13

1 *Nevada* (Battleship)

2 *Arizona* (Battleship)

3 *Vestal* (Repair Ship)

4 *Tennessee* (Battleship)

5 *West Virginia* (Battleship)

6 *Maryland* (Battleship)

7 *Oklahoma* (Battleship)

8 *Neosho* (Oiler)

9 *California* (Battleship)

10 *Raleigh* (Light Cruiser)

11 *Utah* (Target Ship)

12 *Ogala* (Minelayer)

13 *Helena* (Light Cruiser)

## JAPANESE FORCES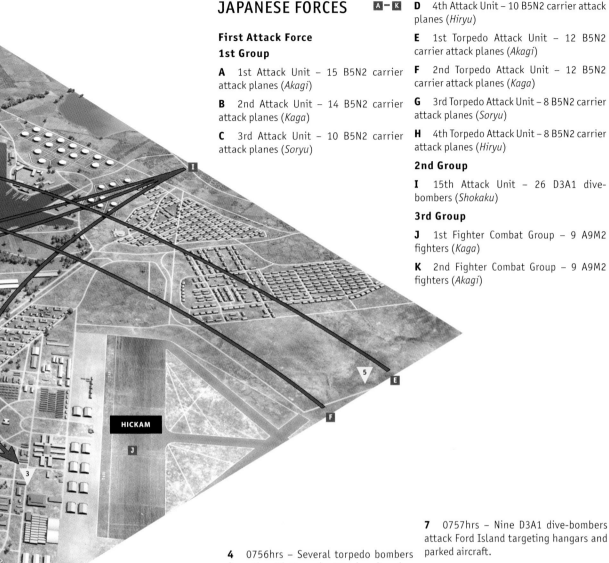

### First Attack Force

### 1st Group

**A** 1st Attack Unit – 15 B5N2 carrier attack planes (*Akagi*)

**B** 2nd Attack Unit – 14 B5N2 carrier attack planes (*Kaga*)

**C** 3rd Attack Unit – 10 B5N2 carrier attack planes (*Soryu*)

**D** 4th Attack Unit – 10 B5N2 carrier attack planes (*Hiryu*)

**E** 1st Torpedo Attack Unit – 12 B5N2 carrier attack planes (*Akagi*)

**F** 2nd Torpedo Attack Unit – 12 B5N2 carrier attack planes (*Kaga*)

**G** 3rd Torpedo Attack Unit – 8 B5N2 carrier attack planes (*Soryu*)

**H** 4th Torpedo Attack Unit – 8 B5N2 carrier attack planes (*Hiryu*)

### 2nd Group

**I** 15th Attack Unit – 26 D3A1 dive-bombers (*Shokaku*)

### 3rd Group

**J** 1st Fighter Combat Group – 9 A9M2 fighters (*Kaga*)

**K** 2nd Fighter Combat Group – 9 A9M2 fighters (*Akagi*)

## ▼ EVENTS

**1** 0750hrs – Commander Fuchida gives order to attack.

**2** 0755hrs – 3rd and 4th Torpedo Attack Units commence attack on ships berthed on the west side of Ford Island. *Soryu's* torpedo bombers hit *Raleigh* once. *Hiryu's* 4th Torpedo Attack Unit scores two hits on *Utah* which causes her to capsize at 0810hrs.

**3** 0755hrs – The bulk of the 2nd Group (17 D3A1 dive-bombers) attack Hickam Field.

**4** 0756hrs – Several torpedo bombers from the 4th Torpedo Attack unit swing south along Ford Island and attack units moored at the 1010 Pier. One torpedo hits *Helena* at 0757hrs; minelayer *Ogala* moored next to *Helena* is damaged below the waterline and later sinks 1000hrs.

**5** 0756hrs – 1st and 2nd Torpedo Attack Units approach Battleship Row from the southeast.

**6** 0757hrs – Many of the torpedoes launched against Battleship Row find their targets. The Japanese claim nine hits on *West Virginia* and *Oklahoma*; though the actual count is less, both ships sink quickly. Two torpedoes hit *California* and she eventually settles on the bottom of the harbor. *Nevada* takes a single hit, but this causes severe flooding.

**7** 0757hrs – Nine D3A1 dive-bombers attack Ford Island targeting hangars and parked aircraft.

**8** 0803hrs – Torpedo hits *Nevada*.

**9** 0805hrs – The 49 B5N2s of the 1st Group acting as level bombers begin their attack from the south.

**10** 0805hrs – First torpedo hit on *California*.

**11** 0811hrs – A single bomb, likely from a *Hiryu* aircraft, penetrates the forward magazine of *Arizona*, creating an explosion which destroys the battleship and damages *Vestal* moored alongside. Other bomb hits are scored on *California*, *Maryland* and *Tennessee*.

**12** Fighter cover is provided by 18 A6M2 fighters from *Kaga* and *Akagi* which are also tasked to strafe aircraft on Ford Island and Hickam Field.

confirmed that no carriers were present, but no effort was made to change the basic attack plan.

The pilots of the torpedo planes faced the greatest challenge of any of the Japanese raiders; their skill was pivotal. Both air speed and drop altitude were critical if the Type 91 torpedoes were to hit the water at the proper water entry angle. As the pilots approached the harbor, each had just seconds to make several critical decisions. First, he had to identify the correct target. Then the correct range was required, since the torpedo needed at least 650ft to arm itself. Most importantly, the correct speed and altitude had to be achieved; the altitude aspect was especially challenging since the aircraft's altimeter was not reliable at extremely low altitudes. If the drop was too high, the torpedo would dive into the mud of the harbor bottom. If the torpedo was dropped too low and too fast, it would skip on the surface of the water and break up. The difficulty in this endeavor was amply demonstrated during the November 4 dress rehearsal when only 40 percent of the torpedo planes simulated their drop at the correct altitude. Nevertheless, because of the intensive training of the aircrews, Japanese planners expected that of 40 torpedoes dropped, 27 would hit their targets.

By the time the torpedo bombers made their final runs, the attack had already started as a result of the dive-bombers confusing Fuchida's attack signal. Each of the groups of Murata's aircraft approached the target area in single-line formations with the goal of about 1,000ft between aircraft, though in reality they were more strung out. This allowed each aircraft a clear run to the target, but it also allowed the defenders to engage each aircraft sequentially once they recovered from their initial surprise. Since they had a more direct route to the target, the torpedo attack opened at 0755hrs with *Soryu*'s and *Hiryu*'s 16 aircraft against the ships anchored on the northwest side of Ford Island. These aircraft were given the mission of hitting the carriers which pre-strike intelligence indicted normally moored on this side of the island. The attackers knew that none were present the day before, but hoped that a carrier had arrived before the attack. However, on

This is a view of Battleship Row taken by a Japanese aircraft in the early stages of the attack. The time is about 0800hrs as the torpedo planes are in the process of doing their work, but the level bombers have not yet made their appearance. Seen from lower left to right are *Nevada*, *Arizona* with repair ship *Vestal* outboard, *Tennessee* with *West Virginia* outboard, *Maryland* with *Oklahoma* outboard, oiler *Neosho*, and finally *California*. *West Virginia*, *Oklahoma*, and *California* have already been torpedoed, marked by ripples and spreading oil, and the first two are listing to port. Splashes from torpedo drops and torpedo tracks are visible at left and center. The smoke in the center is from the torpedoed light cruiser *Helena*. The heavier smoke in the distance is from Hickam Field, which has already been attacked by dive-bombers. (Naval History and Heritage Command)

this morning of December 7 these 16 torpedo aircraft were faced with a dilemma that they did not handle well. Some of the berths on the northwest side of Ford Island were vacant and the only ships moored were the training ship *Utah*, the light cruisers *Raleigh* and *Detroit*, and the seaplane tender *Tangier*. None of these ships were worth the expenditure of a precious torpedo. Nevertheless, the first aircraft to reach the target, the eight Type 97s from *Soryu*, led by Lieutenant Nagai Tsuyoshi, began attack runs against these secondary

targets. Though Nagai and his wingman recognized these targets as low value, the other six *Soryu* aircraft continued their attack runs and each dropped its torpedo. The first passed forward of the former battleship *Utah* and hit the light cruiser *Raleigh*; the second hit *Utah*; the third hit Ford Island near the light cruiser *Detroit*; the fourth failed to hit anything and its fate remains unknown; the fifth hit the shore near *Raleigh*; and the final torpedo hit forward on *Utah*. *Utah* was a former battleship, so this could explain the misidentification on the part of the Japanese. *Utah* had been demilitarized and no longer possessed its belt armor. It was hit by two torpedoes and capsized by 0812hrs. Sixty-four of the ship's crew were killed and the wreck of the ship still remains where it was sunk. *Raleigh* was hit by a single torpedo that flooded the forward engine room and two fire rooms. Quick counterflooding and jettisoning of all movable topside weight saved it from capsizing as well.

Nagai was not fooled by *Utah*'s appearance and decided to expend his ordnance at a better target. He flew around Ford Island intending to look for a more valuable target at the 1010 Pier in the Navy Yard. The battleship *Pennsylvania* was known to often berth there. He saw a large ship at the pier, made his attack run and released his torpedo. Instead of *Pennsylvania*, he was actually dropping his torpedo against the ancient minelayer *Oglala* moored outboard from the modern light cruiser *Helena*. His torpedo ran under *Oglala* and hit *Helena* where it flooded one boiler room and one engine room. The shock of the explosion split open the hull of *Oglala* and it began to take on water before capsizing two hours later. Nagai's wingman recognized *Helena* as a cruiser, so he did not attack. He pulled up to circle around and drop against a high-value target on Battleship Row.

Confusion reigned from the start as *Hiryu*'s aircraft approached the target area. Six of the eight aircraft missed the turn of the rest of the formation and briefly circled near Ewa Field. Two other aircraft, led by *Hiryu*'s torpedo attack leader Lieutenant Matsumura Hirata, quickly determined there were no worthwhile targets located to the northwest of Ford Island and turned south to come around to attack Battleship Row. When the other six *Hiryu* aircraft showed up, they saw Nagai's successful attack against targets moored

This low-quality photograph of the western side of Ford Island, taken by a Japanese aircraft, shows the results of the torpedo attacks. From left to right are light cruiser *Detroit*, light cruiser *Raleigh* (listing to port after being hit by one torpedo), training ship *Utah* (already capsized after being hit by two torpedoes), and seaplane tender *Tangier*. (Naval History and Heritage Command)

OVERLEAF: Battleship Row during the attack by Lieutenant Commander Murata's torpedo bombers. On the right is battleship *Oklahoma* and to the left is *West Virginia*. Behind them are *Maryland* and *Tennessee* respectively. Of the 12 aircraft in *Akagi*'s torpedo bomber unit, 11 dropped their torpedoes. The results were devastating. As *Oklahoma* was the easiest target to approach, it took the brunt of the attack, and was hit by several torpedoes. Here, it has already started to list to port.

This view of Battleship Row, taken by a Type 97 carrier attack plane operating as a level bomber, shows the early phases of the horizontal bombing attack. Ships seen are (from left to right) *Nevada*, *Arizona* with *Vestal* moored outboard, *Tennessee* with *West Virginia* moored outboard, and *Maryland* with *Oklahoma* moored outboard. The white areas on some of the battleships are awnings rigged to protect crews from the tropical heat. The stern of oiler *Neosho* is barely visible at the extreme right. A bomb has just hit *Arizona* at the stern, but it has not yet received the bomb that detonated its forward magazines. *West Virginia* and *Oklahoma* are gushing oil from their many torpedo hits and are listing to port. *Oklahoma*'s port deck edge is already under water. *Nevada* has also been torpedoed. (Naval History and Heritage Command)

at the 1010 Pier, and they turned to join in. Two of the aircraft broke off, but the other four each launched their torpedoes. All missed, with one hitting the pier and the other three hitting the bottom of the harbor. This disappointing result can be explained by the fact that the Americans had taken these aircraft under fire, but probably more by the reflection and glare from the sun, which was directly ahead. This left four *Hiryu* and one *Soryu* torpedo bomber yet to drop their weapons and all were maneuvering to get into position to attack Battleship Row.

Leading the attack were the 12 carrier attack planes from *Akagi* led by Murata. These approached in a long line-ahead formation with over 1,600ft between aircraft, extending to as much as 6,000ft separation in the latter half of the formation. Directly in front of them were the two outboard battleships *Oklahoma* and *West Virginia*. Starting at 0757hrs with Murata's drop, the first six *Akagi* torpedo planes targeted these two ships, scoring several hits in quick succession. The first two aircraft of *Akagi*'s final flight of six veered left to attack *California*, scoring one hit. One aircraft attacked *West Virginia*, and the final three took the easiest target, *Oklahoma*. The Japanese claim that 11 *Akagi* carrier attack planes dropped their torpedoes (one jettisoned its torpedo as the result of a near air-to-air collision), and that all 11 hit one of the three battleships targeted. Interspersed among the final six *Akagi* torpedo bombers were the four remaining *Hiryu* aircraft. The first two of these launched at *West Virginia* and the final two selected *Oklahoma*.

Trailing the *Akagi* torpedo group by three miles were the 12 aircraft from *Kaga*. By now, the volume of antiaircraft fire directed at the slow torpedo planes increased as each approached the target area in succession. None of the other torpedo planes from the other three carriers were shot down, but five of 12 *Kaga* torpedo bombers were destroyed. The first three aircraft dropped against *West Virginia*, and the next two targeted *Oklahoma*. The sixth was hit by antiaircraft fire, jettisoned its torpedo, and crashed on the grounds of the Naval Hospital. The seventh aircraft to attack was also subjected to heavy defensive fire. The torpedo aboard this aircraft was hit, and the aircraft blown up. The next aircraft launched against *West Virginia*. After aborting an earlier attempt to make an attack run against Battleship Row, the final aircraft from

*Soryu* now entered the stream of *Kaga* aircraft. This aircraft successfully launched against *California*, hitting its target, but was heavily damaged by antiaircraft fire. The skillful pilot made it back to the Japanese task force where it was forced to ditch next to a destroyer after its landing gear failed. The *Soryu* aircraft blocked the approach of the ninth *Kaga* aircraft; this aircraft was forced to veer to the right and launched its torpedo on *Nevada*. The torpedo hit the battleship forward, but was shot down. The next aircraft targeted *Oklahoma*. The last two were both shot down before either could launch its torpedo. Of the 12 *Kaga* aircraft, eight dropped their torpedoes against three different battleships; the Japanese claimed all eight hit their target.

The torpedo attack had lasted just 11 minutes. In this time, the Japanese inflicted the most significant damage of the entire attack. For a cost of five aircraft (and a sixth later forced to ditch), torpedoes had sunk two battleships and inflicted damage leading to the sinking of two others. Additionally, a target ship and a minelayer had been sunk and two light cruisers damaged. Of the 36 torpedoes launched, the best available assessment of the number of hits is 19 – just over half. While it is hard to quarrel with these results, the attack had the potential to be even more devastating. As has been described, the attack was not executed smoothly, and the pilots concentrated on the easy targets of *Oklahoma* and *West Virginia* at the expense of other ships. The attack formation selected was also an error and resulted in heavy losses for the last group of aircraft to attack.

## The Horizontal Bombing Attack

The second part of the Japanese double-punch against Battleship Row was the 49 level bombers under the direct command of Fuchida. High hopes were associated with this attack method after intensive practice proved it was a viable means of attacking heavily armored battleships. On this day, ten hits were scored out of 49 bombs dropped for a high hit ratio of 20 percent; this was a better result than expected by Japanese planners. However, of the ten hits, six failed to explode or resulted in only a low order detonation. Overall, the results were disappointing with the horizontal bombers missing *California* and *Nevada*, placing two ineffective hits on *Maryland*, and achieving hits on *West Virginia* and *Tennessee*. However, all of this was overshadowed by the two hits on the unfortunate *Arizona*, one of which resulted in a magazine explosion. This single devastating hit became the iconic event of the entire attack.

Fuchida had instructed his pilots to make as many passes as necessary to ensure good results. The 49 horizontal bombers approached Battleship Row from the south at 10,000ft in groups of five. Each of the ten groups was separated by 600ft, with the first group of four aircraft led by Fuchida himself. In his account of the battle, his group was aiming at *Nevada* at the end of Battleship Row, but at the last instant clouds obscured the target. Fuchida ordered the group to bank right and come around again. The second time he targeted battleship *Maryland* and claimed two hits and two near misses. Subsequent analysis confirms that in reality all of the bombs from Fuchida's group missed. Fuchida than remained over Pearl Harbor for the remainder of the attack to observe results.

This vertical view of Battleship Row, taken by a Type 97 carrier attack plane, was taken right after the deadly bomb hit on *Arizona* that resulted in a magazine explosion and the ship's destruction. From left to right are *Nevada*, *Arizona* (burning intensely) with *Vestal* moored outboard, *Tennessee* with *West Virginia* moored outboard, and *Maryland* with the capsized *Oklahoma* alongside. Smoke from bomb hits on *Vestal* and *West Virginia* is also visible. (Naval History and Heritage Command)

The iconic image of the attack was the destruction of battleship *Arizona*. This image was taken at the moment the ship's forward magazine exploded after being hit by an 800kg bomb. (Naval History and Heritage Command)

## Agony on Battleship Row

In only a few minutes, the Japanese had inflicted devastating damage on Battleship Row. Worst off was *Oklahoma*. A total of 12 torpedoes were launched at it and of these at least five hit their target. It took three torpedoes in quick succession and immediately began to heel to port. A fourth torpedo hit accelerated its heeling action. This, coupled with the fact that the ship's anti-torpedo voids had their inspection covers removed, compromising their watertight integrity, meant that the ship capsized in 15 minutes. The damage was incurred so quickly that no attempt was made to counterflood. The order to abandon ship was quickly given, but personnel losses were still high. The final cost was 20 officers and 395 enlisted men dead, with another 32 wounded out of the ship's crew on December 1 of 82 officers and 1,272 enlisted. Thirty-two men were saved by heroic sailors and dock workers cutting through hull in the hours and days after the attack.

The forward magazine explosion sank *Arizona* and caused an intense fire that engulfed the forward part of the ship as shown here. At left, crewmen on the stern of *Tennessee* are using fire hoses to keep burning oil away from their ship. (Naval History and Heritage Command)

Moored inboard from *Oklahoma* was *Maryland*. This position saved it from major damage. Of all the ships on Battleship Row, it was the least damaged. The ship was hit by a single 800kg bomb on the forecastle below the waterline. Another bomb hit the forecastle but caused little damage. Of its crew on December 1 of 108 officers and 1,496 enlisted, only two officers and two enlisted men were killed with another 14 wounded.

Moored aft of Oklahoma and *Maryland* were *West Virginia* and

*Tennessee*. As the outboard ship, *West Virginia* took the most punishment. It was hit in the opening minutes by probably seven torpedoes. After the first torpedo hits, the ship took a 22° list. As it was rolling, it was hit by two more torpedoes, probably from *Hiryu* aircraft. Orders from quick-reacting junior officers to flood voids on the starboard side were issued and this prompt decision brought the ship from a 28° degree to a 15° list. This allowed it to settle and avoid capsizing. This, and quick orders to send the crew to General Quarters, saved many lives. In addition, the ship was hit by an 800kg bomb that penetrated the main deck and wrecked the port casemates. By 0940hrs fire engulfed the ship from its bow to Turret Number 1. At 1005hrs the word was given to abandon ship since there was no power to fight the fires that now engulfed the superstructure. These fires were not controlled until that afternoon when fire parties returned to the ship. Of its December 1 crew of 87 officers and 1,454 men, two officers and 103 enlisted personnel were killed and another 52 wounded. Among the dead was the ship's commanding officer, who was hit by a splinter from a bomb that exploded on the adjacent *Tennessee*. He continued to fight despite his mortal abdominal wounds and for this he was awarded a posthumous Medal of Honor.

Moored inboard of *West Virginia* was *Tennessee*. It took two 800kg bombs early in the attack, but suffered little damage. The first hit the center gun of Turret Number 2; the second pierced the roof of Turret Number 3 but broke apart without detonating. Most damage came from the fires started by debris and burning oil from *Arizona* moored only 75ft aft. Only five men were killed and another 21 wounded out of a total of 94 officers and 1,372 men onboard on December 1. The ship was wedged against the mooring station and the sunken *West Virginia* but was underway by December 20.

Just aft of *Tennessee* was *Arizona* with repair ship *Vestal* moored alongside. Two 800kg bombs hit the battleship, the first hitting aft on the quarterdeck. The second, striking at 0809hrs, penetrated the forward 14in gun magazine, which resulted in a cataclysmic explosion. This single blast killed some 1,000 of the ship's crew and utterly destroyed the forward part of the ship. Heavy fires resulted, which burned for days.

Aircraft from *Hiryu* were responsible for this destruction. The final casualty count was 47 officers and 1,056 enlisted killed, and another five officers and 39 enlisted wounded out of its December 1 crew of 100 officers and 1,411 enlisted personnel. Among the dead were the ship's captain and the embarked admiral commanding a division of battleships; both were posthumously awarded the Medal of

DECEMBER 7
1941

0854hrs
Second wave given
order to attack

A motor launch rescues survivors from the water alongside the sunken *West Virginia* during the attack. Note the extensive distortion of *West Virginia*'s lower amidships superstructure, which was caused by torpedoes that exploded high up on the hull. Also note the CXAM radar antenna atop *West Virginia*'s foremast. *Tennessee* is inboard of the sunken battleship. (Naval History and Heritage Command)

Honor. *Vestal* took two bomb hits; the first hit forward and penetrated three decks before exploding in a storage compartment, and the second sliced through the ship creating a 3ft by 5ft hole in its side. *Vestal* was down by the stern and took a starboard list. It got underway at 0845hrs with the assistance of tugs, and beached on Aiea Shoal to keep from sinking.

*Nevada* was moored in an exposed position at the end of Battleship Row. At 0803hrs it was hit by a torpedo on its port bow that created a large 48ft by 33ft hole. It was undamaged in the ensuing horizontal bombing attack. Burning oil from the shattered *Arizona* directly in front threatened to engulf the ship, so the order was given to get underway. Power did not permit this until 0840hrs when it backed down before beginning to move down the channel between the Navy Yard and Ford Island. This coincided with the arrival of the second attack wave.

The last battleship moored on Battleship Row was *California*, positioned in the southeasternmost spot. Its watertight integrity was compromised in preparation for an inspection the next day. Two torpedoes hit the ship; one struck forward of the bridge below its armored belt and the other also struck down low, below Turret Number 3. The ship started to capsize but counterflooding corrected this. Power was lost at about the same time as the torpedo hits, but was brought back on line at 0855hrs, allowing the fires to be fought successfully. Burning oil engulfed the ship's stern and at 1002hrs the crew was ordered to abandon ship; this was rescinded at 1015hrs after the blazes subsided. An examination after the attack indicated that the ship should not have sunk as the result of two torpedo hits, but that its loss was the result of poor watertight integrity and human error. *California* continued to settle slowly until it rested on the bottom of the harbor on December 10. Six officers and 92 enlisted men were killed; another three officers and 58 enlisted were wounded from its December 1 crew of 120 officers and 1,546 enlisted.

## Attacks Against Airfields

The American air installation closest to the oncoming Japanese strike was Wheeler Field, located in the center of the island. This was the Hawaiian Air Force's primary fighter base with some 140 fighter aircraft (87 P-40B/C, 39 P-36 and 12 P-26) of which 82 were operational. On November 27 the base commander was ordered to remove his fighters from the 125 protective revetments on base and line them up on the apron for easier guarding. Pleas to return the aircraft to their revetments were refused because of claims that it would excite the local population. In order to neutralize this threat, *Zuikaku*'s entire force of 25 dive-bombers was allocated against targets on Wheeler Field. Beginning at 0751hrs, *Zuikaku*'s dive-bombers demonstrated the folly of the lack of defensive prudence. The aircraft came in from the north and then swung to the west to begin their dives. Against no antiaircraft fire, direct hits were scored on Hangars 1 and 3, and the barracks of the 6th Pursuit Squadron was hit. The dive-bombers pressed their attacks down to 500–1,000ft and proved very accurate in their delivery. The 120 fighters parked on the apron were also targeted. At 0755hrs, eight fighters from *Soryu* followed up with first of three strafing passes.

Planes and hangars burning at Wheeler Army Airfield. This view is from an attacking Japanese aircraft, probably a dive-bomber from *Zuikaku*. (Naval History and Heritage Command)

Kaneohe Naval Air Station, located on the east side of Oahu, was the next air facility struck. The base was the home of Patrol Wing 1 with three squadrons (VP-11, 12, 14) with 36 total aircraft. Of these, 33 were present; four were moored in the bay with four located in Hangar 1 and 25 on the apron. Beginning at 0753hrs, Kaneohe came under attack by fighters from *Shokaku* and *Zuikaku*. In eight minutes, all of the aircraft in the open were destroyed or damaged. With no antiaircraft protection at the base, the Japanese fighters executed repeated strafing passes using their 20mm guns until they ran out of ammunition.

Ewa Mooring Mast Field was the home of Marine Air Group 21 with three subordinate squadrons with 49 assigned aircraft. This facility also came under attack at 0753hrs when six *Hiryu* fighters began their strafing attacks. They were followed from 0805 to 0820hrs by eight *Soryu* fighters, which continued to strafe the base and intercepted the *Enterprise* dive-bombers that attempted to land in the middle of the attack. The onslaught concluded with *Shokaku* dive-bombers, and *Akagi* and *Kaga* fighters strafing the base from 0815 to 0830hrs after they had conducted their primary attacks.

A PBY patrol aircraft burning at Kaneohe Naval Air Station. The three patrol squadrons based at Kaneohe were virtually annihilated in the attack. (Naval History and Heritage Command)

Most of the 12 B-17 bombers that arrived in the middle of the attack survived the experience. Shown here is a B-17E at Hickam Airfield after landing safely. In the background is a B-17C/D. Smoke from burning ships at Pearl Harbor is visible in the distance. (Naval History and Heritage Command)

The parked aircraft suffered heavily, and by the end of the attack over half were in flames. Personnel losses were remarkably light with only four dead.

The attack against Ford Island Naval Air Station started at 0755hrs. Minutes later, this base issued the first report of the raid to the world with its famous report: "Air Raid Pearl Harbor. This is not a drill." Ford Island was home to two patrol squadrons and was the temporary base for aircraft from carriers moored in port. To neutralize this threat, nine dive-bombers from *Shokaku* were used. These did great damage to the hangars and accounted for a great many aircraft destroyed. When the *Arizona* blew up minutes into the attack, the explosion destroyed the water main, leaving the base with minimal fire-fighting capability.

Nearby Hickam Field was the Hawaiian Air Force's main bomber base. As such, it was a critical component of the Japanese plans to cripple American air power. The base had its primary striking power of 12 B-17s, 32 B-18s, and 12 A-20s lined up in rows just 10ft apart in accordance with Short's anti-sabotage plans. The bulk of *Shokaku*'s dive-bombers were allocated against this important target. At 0755hrs, about half of the 17 dive-bombers attacked from the east, with the remainder attacking from the north; their primary targets were the hangars and the aircraft lined up on the apron. This was followed at 0800hrs by nine *Akagi* fighters from the southeast to strafe the aircraft on the hangar line. These aircraft made three passes before departing at 0810hrs to strafe nearby Ewa to the west. At 0805hrs, nine *Kaga* fighters joined the attack. Heavy damage was inflicted on the hangars and the nearby large barracks building was also bombed.

Adding to the confusion, two groups of American aircraft arrived in the middle of the attack. At 0615hrs carrier *Enterprise*, located about 215 miles due west of Oahu, launched 18 Dauntless dive-bombers to conduct patrols in front of the ship. The aircraft were ordered to recover at Ford Island and were not carrying bombs. The lead two aircraft arrived during the raid and, though attacked by Japanese fighters and American antiaircraft fire, both landed safely at Ford Island. The other 16 arrived in pairs, and only one was able to land at Ford Island. Three were shot down by Japanese fighters and another two destroyed by friendly antiaircraft fire. Seven finally landed at Ewa Field and another at Hickam. One went to a field on Kauai.

Also during the early stages of the attack, a flight of 12 B-17 heavy bombers (eight B-17E and four B-17C) from the 38th and 88th Reconnaissance Squadrons (Heavy) arrived over Hickam. The aircraft had just completed a long flight from the continental United States and each carried only a skeleton crew of five and was unarmed. Despite the attention immediately devoted to the newcomers by Japanese fighters, few of the

DECEMBER 7
1941

0855hrs
Kaneohe
attacked

aircraft were lost. One B-17C was strafed while landing at Hickam and burned out, and another was landed in a golf course in northern Oahu. Seven landed at Hickam between attacks, two at Haleiwa and one at Bellows. Despite damage, most were ready to fly the next day.

## The Saga of the Midget Submarines

The five midget submarines committed to the Hawaii operation were considered to be a top-secret weapon originally designed to take part in the decisive battle between the US and Imperial fleets. The Type A midget submarine was 78.5ft long and had a submerged displacement of 46 tons. Each submarine was heavily armed with two 17.7in torpedoes. However, they suffered from a short range. The 600 horsepower electric motor could make 23 knots surfaced or 19 knots submerged but endurance was limited to 80nm at 6 knots or 100nm at 2 knots.

During the October 4–5, 1941 planning conference to discuss the details of the Pearl Harbor operation, those involved with the midget submarine program proposed using the craft to attack the Pacific Fleet in harbor. By October 11–13, Yamamoto approved the proposal and gave it the name *Shinki* (Divine Turtle) Operation Number 1. This was in spite of the strong opposition of the aviators on his staff who feared that the early detection of the midget submarines entering the harbor would jeopardize the security of the entire operation. Yamamoto was not fazed by their arguments, and work began immediately on modifying five midget submarines with increased harbor-penetration capabilities. This work was finished on November 10, and all five midget submarines were loaded on their mother submarines for the trip to Pearl Harbor.

On the morning of December 7, all five mother submarines had made the transit undetected to a position just south of Pearl Harbor. Between 0042 and 0333hrs that morning, all five were launched. Even 70 years later there remain several key questions as to the operations of the midget submarines, but some things are clear. The fears of the Japanese aviators were proved well founded when at least one of the submarines was detected some time before the air attack was to begin. Fortunately for the Japanese, the Americans failed to take advantage of this potentially critical warning. Furthermore, all five midget submarines were lost, and it appears that they contributed nothing in the process. Compared to the potential contributions of the air attack, five midget submarines could contribute little, so the possible loss of surprise was not worth the gamble taken by Yamamoto to include them in the operation.

An irony of the Pearl Harbor attack was that the Americans fired the first shot of the battle. This is destroyer *Ward*'s Number 3 4in gun and its crew. At 0637hrs *Ward* sighted a submarine and engaged it minutes later with gunfire. The early discovery of a midget submarine attempting to enter the harbor was the worst nightmare of the Japanese aviators since it threatened the surprise of the air attack. Despite the potential of over one hour's notice before the air attack, the Americans were still caught totally by surprise. (Naval History and Heritage Command)

The second of the five midget submarines recovered after the attack was the one sunk by destroyer *Monaghan* inside the harbor. The effect of the destroyer's ramming and depth charge attack can easily be seen on the hull of the midget. The hulk was subsequently buried in a landfill. (Naval History and Heritage Command)

Divine Turtle Operation Number 1 started off poorly when at 0342hrs minesweeper *Condor* spotted what appeared to be a submarine in the restricted area south of the channel into the harbor. By 0408hrs destroyer *Ward* arrived in the area to prosecute the contact report but could find nothing. At 0630hrs, stores ship *Antares* spotted the sub which was later marked by a PBY flying boat. *Ward* was now able to establish contact, and opened fire at 0645hrs. Its first shot missed, but the second hit the submarine at the base of its sail. *Ward* dropped depth charges to ensure the sub's destruction. Having engaged an apparently hostile submarine, *Ward* sent the signal at 0651hrs: "WE HAVE ATTACKED FIRED UPON AND DROPPED DEPTH CHARGES UPON SUBMARINE OPERATING IN DEFENSE SEA AREA." This was not acted upon, perhaps because of the many submarine contact reports issued over the past weeks, just another sign of the lack of battle readiness demonstrated by the Americans. In 2002 the submarine sunk by *Ward* was found, five miles off Pearl Harbor, complete with the 4in shell hole readily discernable in its sail.

Another submarine experienced gyroscope problems and got lost. It was found the next morning on a beach near Bellows Field, where one of its crew was captured. This submarine is now on display in Texas. A third submarine was discovered in 1960 in the Keehi Lagoon off the entrance to Pearl Harbor. This submarine had its two torpedoes still on board.

At least one of the midget submarines did succeed in penetrating into the harbor. At 0836hrs personnel aboard seaplane tender *Curtiss* spotted a submarine several hundred yards off its starboard quarter. A number of ships in the area began to engage the target with gunfire. The midget fired one of its torpedoes at *Curtiss*, but missed. After firing, the submarine broached, and then was hit by a 5in shell from *Curtiss*.

Meanwhile, destroyer *Monaghan*, which had gotten underway a few minutes earlier, continued to close the submarine with the intent to ram. The midget submarine responded by turning to face the destroyer and fired its second torpedo. It missed the oncoming destroyer some 20–30 yards off its portside. At 0844hrs, *Monaghan* rammed the submarine and dropped depth charges as it ran over the submarine. This submarine was raised off the harbor floor two weeks later.

The fate of the fifth midget is almost certainly related to an incident involving light cruiser *St. Louis* while it was clearing the harbor channel just after 1000hrs. Crewmen aboard the cruiser sighted a midget submarine that fired two torpedoes 2,000 yards off the ship's starboard beam. One of the torpedoes struck a coral reef 200 yards from the ship and exploded; the explosion apparently accounted for the second following torpedo. Between 1004 and 1007hrs *St. Louis* directed 5in gunfire at the submarine, which was followed by destroyer *Blue* gaining sonar contact and delivering a depth charge attack.

## The Second Attack Force

The 167 aircraft of the second wave were led by Lieutenant Commander Shimazaki Shigekazu from *Zuikaku*. For the second wave, no torpedo planes were included; carrier attack planes only would act as level bombers against the airfields. These 54 bombers were divided into three groups to attack Ford Island and Kanoehe Naval Air Stations and Hickam Field. The large force of 78 dive-bombers was tasked to engage carriers and cruisers in and around the Naval Yard and Ford Island. Thirty-five fighters were divided into two groups, one targeted against Hickam and the other against targets on the eastern part of the island, principally Kanoehe and Bellows Field. The attack group approached from the north and slipped around the east side of Oahu. At 0854hrs Shimazaki gave the order to attack.

The lead aircraft of the second wave arrived over their targets approximately 25 minutes after the last aircraft of the first wave had departed. The centerpiece of the Second Attack Force was the 78 dive-bombers from the carriers *Akagi*, *Kaga*, *Soryu*, and *Hiryu*. These were the best dive-bomber pilots in the Imperial Navy and they had scored impressively during exercises against moving targets. Against stationary ships in Pearl Harbor, much was expected. They were led by the famous dive-bomber pilot Lieutenant Commander Egusa Takashige from *Soryu*.

## Attack of the Dive-bombers

Since there were no carriers present, the next priority target for the dive-bombers was cruisers. Battleships were the third priority, but since the Type 99s were only carrying 250kg bombs, these were unsuited for attacking such heavily armored ships. What resulted was a generally chaotic attack that produced minimal additional damage to that already inflicted by the first wave. Japanese after-action reports were inaccurate at best and misleading at worst, so the activities of the 78 dive-bombers have to be reconstructed using American after-action reports. While even these cannot account for all 78 aircraft,

OVERLEAF: *Ward* engaging a Japanese midget submarine attempting to enter Pearl Harbor on the morning of December 7. Alerted by other ships and a patrol aircraft, *Ward* spotted the sail of the unknown submarine and closed for an attack. At 0645hrs it engaged the target. The first shot of the war was fired by *Ward*'s Number 1 mount, which missed from a range of about 100 yards. A second shot from the Number 3 mount at about 50 yards was seen to strike the sail and cause the small submarine to heel over. *Ward* then dropped depth charges as the submarine dove below the surface. The wreck was discovered in 1,200ft of water in August 2002.

A Type 99 carrier bomber pulling up after delivering its bomb as part of the second attack wave. The results of the dive-bomber attack were disappointing for the Japanese. (Naval History and Heritage Command)

they do confirm that the dive-bomber attack was unfocused and failed to attack proper targets. Some 30 aircraft selected battleships as targets and another 17 attacked cruisers, but as many as 16 attacked destroyers and 12 attacked auxiliaries.

Of the 30 attacks on battleships, the majority were against *Nevada* as it moved down the channel to the harbor entrance. At about 0850hrs, just as the dive-bombers arrived at Pearl Harbor, *Nevada* was underway and was located in the channel on the east side of Ford Island. Such a target proved too tempting for the Japanese to resist. They immediately concentrated their effort against it with between 14 and 18 dive-bombers, which attacked the slowly moving battleship. Within minutes, *Nevada* was surrounded by near-misses before it was hit by five bombs at 0900hrs. At 0907hrs more dive-bombers, including some from *Kaga*, pressed the attack and scored another hit. The torpedo hit earlier on *Nevada* had created a small list to port and made the ship down by the bow. The Japanese dive-bombers placed a minimum of three bombs forward of Turret Number 1, which opened more holes in the bow and started fires that burned out of control. In response the forward magazines were flooded, which brought the bow down further. Another bomb hit between the stack and the superstructure, and another between the stack and the mainmast. Under orders from Admiral Kimmel at 0910hrs, *Nevada* ran aground at Hospital Point. At 1030hrs it was dragged across the channel by tugs. Of the ship's crew on December 1 of 94 officers and 1,390 enlisted men, three officers and 47 men were killed in the attack with another 109 wounded.

Despite Japanese claims that the dive-bombers added another 21 bomb hits to targets on Battleship Row, the only actual attack was against *California*. At 0845hrs, between one and three dive-bombers attacked the battleship, scoring a single hit on the starboard upper deck next to a 5in gun mount. The bomb penetrated to the second deck, where it exploded causing many casualties and a fire. The only other battleship not located in Battleship Row was fleet flagship *Pennsylvania*, located in Dry Dock Number 1. It was undamaged in the first wave, but now it came under attack by as many as nine dive-bombers. At 0906hrs it took a hit by a 250kg bomb on the boat deck, which detonated in a 5in gun casemate. Damage was light but two officers and 16 enlisted men were killed and another 30 wounded. Located in the same dry dock with *Pennsylvania* were destroyers *Cassin* and *Downes*. These suffered heavily from the bombs that were targeted against *Pennsylvania* but fell further forward in the dry dock. Two bombs hit *Cassin*, resulting in burning oil being spread over the two destroyers. An attempt to put the flames out was made by pumping water

The wrecked destroyers *Downes* and *Cassin* in dry dock number one after being struck by dive-bombers in the second wave. *Cassin* has capsized against *Downes*. Battleship *Pennsylvania* occupies the rest of the dry dock. The torpedo-damaged cruiser *Helena* is in the right distance beyond the crane. Visible in the center distance is the capsized *Oklahoma* with *Maryland* alongside. The visible smoke is from the sunken and burning *Arizona*. *California* is partially visible at the extreme left. (Naval History and Heritage Command)

The forward magazine of destroyer *Shaw* exploded as a result of a dive-bombing attack during the second wave. The destroyer was undergoing overhaul in floating dry dock YFD-2. At right is the bow of battleship *Nevada* with a tug alongside fighting fires. (Naval History and Heritage Command)

into the dry dock, but this merely resulted in the flames riding the water. As a result, the heat of the fires ignited the forward magazines. Another bomb hit the bridge of *Downes*. Finally, *Cassin* rolled over on top of *Downes*; both ships were constructive losses.

At least ten dive-bombers focused on the Navy Yard area, presumably attempting to hit the two heavy and two light cruisers present. Egusa himself targeted the heavy cruiser *New Orleans* but missed. Light cruiser *Honolulu* suffered a near miss that opened its hull to the sea. It returned to service within a month. Light cruiser *St. Louis* suffered three near misses but no damage. Another four dive-bombers attacked *Helena* at the 1010 Pier, but caused no damage. The only other cruiser attacked was light cruiser *Raleigh* still struggling to stay afloat from its earlier torpedo damage. As many as five dive-bombers, at least some from *Akagi*, selected it for attack and at 0908hrs scored a hit. The bomb hit the ship under the waterline and pierced the lightly armored hull to explode outside. The ship was again subjected to flooding and

None of the ships located on the western side of Ford Island were valuable targets, but two were attacked. *Raleigh* is being kept from capsizing by a barge lashed alongside after it sustained damage from a torpedo and a bomb. The capsized hull of *Utah* is visible astern of *Raleigh*. (Naval History and Heritage Command)

# SECOND ATTACK WAVE AGAINST TARGETS IN PEARL HARBOR

**0848–0920HRS, DECEMBER 7, 1941**

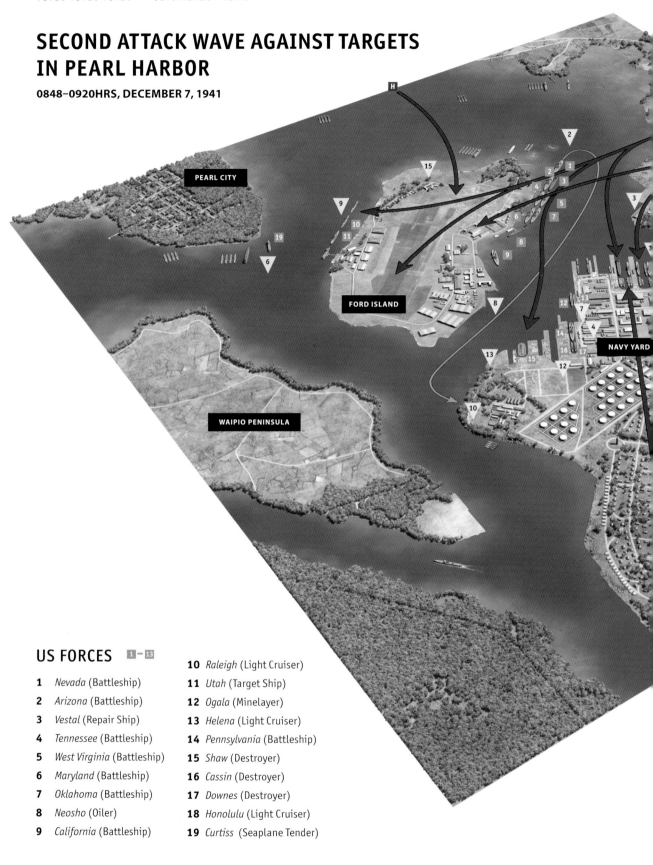

PEARL CITY

FORD ISLAND

WAIPIO PENINSULA

NAVY YARD

## US FORCES 1 – 13

| | | | |
|---|---|---|---|
| **1** | *Nevada* (Battleship) | **10** | *Raleigh* (Light Cruiser) |
| **2** | *Arizona* (Battleship) | **11** | *Utah* (Target Ship) |
| **3** | *Vestal* (Repair Ship) | **12** | *Ogala* (Minelayer) |
| **4** | *Tennessee* (Battleship) | **13** | *Helena* (Light Cruiser) |
| **5** | *West Virginia* (Battleship) | **14** | *Pennsylvania* (Battleship) |
| **6** | *Maryland* (Battleship) | **15** | *Shaw* (Destroyer) |
| **7** | *Oklahoma* (Battleship) | **16** | *Cassin* (Destroyer) |
| **8** | *Neosho* (Oiler) | **17** | *Downes* (Destroyer) |
| **9** | *California* (Battleship) | **18** | *Honolulu* (Light Cruiser) |
| | | **19** | *Curtiss* (Seaplane Tender) |

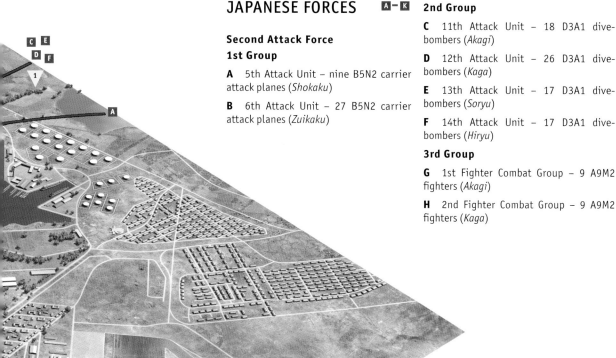

## JAPANESE FORCES A–K

### Second Attack Force

#### 1st Group

**A** 5th Attack Unit – nine B5N2 carrier attack planes (*Shokaku*)

**B** 6th Attack Unit – 27 B5N2 carrier attack planes (*Zuikaku*)

### 2nd Group

**C** 11th Attack Unit – 18 D3A1 dive-bombers (*Akagi*)

**D** 12th Attack Unit – 26 D3A1 dive-bombers (*Kaga*)

**E** 13th Attack Unit – 17 D3A1 dive-bombers (*Soryu*)

**F** 14th Attack Unit – 17 D3A1 dive-bombers (*Hiryu*)

### 3rd Group

**G** 1st Fighter Combat Group – 9 A9M2 fighters (*Akagi*)

**H** 2nd Fighter Combat Group – 9 A9M2 fighters (*Kaga*)

## EVENTS

**1** 0848hrs – 2nd Group approaches Pearl Harbor from the northeast. They are led by the Imperial Navy's acknowledged dive-bombing expert, Lt. Commander Egusa Takashige.

**2** 0850hrs – Battleship *Nevada* gets underway.

**3** 0850hrs – Fuchida sees that *Nevada* is underway and is headed for the channel entrance. He orders Egusa to attack the battleship in order to black the channel. Five quick bomb hits are scored.

**4** 0857hrs – Dive-bombers score hits on *Pennsylvania* and two destroyers in drydock.

**5** 0904hrs – The 5th Attack Unit arrives from the northeast and attacks hangars and aircraft on Ford Island; some aircraft attack *Pennsylvania*.

**6** 0905hrs – A single D3A1 dive-bomber crashes into seaplane tender *Curtiss*, killing 20 crewmen and starting a fire.

**7** 0907hrs – 5th Attack Unit hits *Pennsylvania* with 550lb bomb.

**8** 0907hrs – *Nevada* suffers sixth bomb hit.

**9** 0908hrs – *Raleigh* is attacked by dive-bombers; a single hit does little damage when it passes through the lightly-armored ship.

**10** 0910hrs – *Nevada* intentionally grounds on Hospital Point; she is later towed to the west side of the channel to clear the channel entrance.

**11** 0910hrs – 27 B5N2 level bombers from *Zuikaku* commence attack on hangars and aircraft on Hickam Field. *Akagi's* 1st Fighter Combat Unit strafes the field.

**12** 0912hrs – 6th Attack Unit continues attack on *Pennsylvania* and other targets in the Navy Yard.

**13** 0915hrs – Dive-bombers hit destroyer *Shaw* in floating drydock causing fires and eventually an explosion in the ship's forward magazine.

**14** 0920hrs – A dive-bomber scores a near-miss on *Honolulu* causing underwater damage and flooding.

**15** Fighter cover for Second Attack Force is provided by 18 A6M2 fighters from *Kaga* and *Akagi*. The nine *Kaga* fighters strafe Ford Island and later use their unexpended ordnance against Wheeler Field.

This is a view from the 1010 Pier looking toward the Navy Yard's dry docks. Destroyer *Shaw* in floating dry dock YFD-2 and *Nevada* are burning at right. In the foreground is the capsized minelayer *Oglala* with light cruiser *Helena* further down the pier. Beyond *Helena* is dry dock number one, and the burning destroyers *Cassin* and *Downes*. (Naval History and Heritage Command)

disposed of additional topweight to avoid capsizing. Despite its damage from a torpedo and bomb, it was repaired locally at Pearl Harbor and was again operational by mid-February.

Inexplicably, several destroyers also came under attack. Destroyer *Shaw* was located in the floating dry dock just down from where *Pennsylvania* and the two destroyers shared their dry dock. As many as eight *Akagi* dive-bombers attacked this target at 0912hrs. *Shaw* was hit by three bombs; the third hit passed through the bridge and ruptured its fuel tanks. A serious fire was created and could not be controlled, forcing the ship to be abandoned at 0925hrs. Five minutes later the forward magazine blew up in a spectacular explosion. Other dive-bombers were reported to have attacked destroyers *Dale* and *Helm* while both were underway, but scored no hits.

Two seaplane tenders also came under attack. Both were large ships, but it is hard to understand why they were selected at all. Fire from seaplane tender *Curtiss* hit a dive-bomber over Ford Island at 0905hrs; the crashing aircraft then hit the ship on its starboard side and started a fire. Later, six dive-bombers attacked the ship and a single bomb hit the ship aft in its hangar, causing heavy loss of life (20 killed and 58 wounded) and creating additional fires. The crew put the fire out in 30 minutes. Seaplane tender *Tangier*, moored on the northwest side of Ford Island, was attacked by as many as five dive-bombers but suffered no damage.

For the loss of 14 dive-bombers, Egusa's eagles had made a weak haul. The Japanese claimed 49 hits, but the actual number was probably 15. Though American antiaircraft fire was fairly heavy during this point in the battle, and there was considerable smoke in the harbor area as a result of the burning battleships, the accuracy rate of just under 20 percent against stationary targets was well below expected results. The best explanation would be a 70 to 90 percent low overcast over the harbor by the time the dive-bombers arrived to deliver their attacks. In addition to poor accuracy, the dive-bomber pilots were guilty of poor target selection. According to the pre-attack prioritization plan, and with the absence of any carriers, the primary dive-bombing targets were cruisers. Few pilots adhered to this priority. Lastly, the dive-bomber crews were guilty of gross exaggerations in their post-attack damage-assessment reporting.

## More Attacks Against Airfields

Nine *Shokaku* carrier attack planes acting as horizontal bombers dropped their loads with uncertain results against Ford Island Naval Air Station. Heavy smoke from the burning battleships undoubtedly affected their ability to identify and attack targets. Fighters from *Kaga* briefly strafed targets

before heading for neighboring Hickam Field. At the end of the attack, total losses on Ford Island were 33 aircraft destroyed, including 19 of the base's PBY patrol planes. Most of the damage had been caused by aircraft from the first wave.

At Hickam Field, 27 horizontal bombers from *Zuikaku* escorted by nine fighters from *Akagi* swung in from the south at about 0905hrs to deliver their attacks. The carrier attack planes that were acting as level bombers targeted the hangars and the barracks nearby. This was followed at 0910hrs by three strafing passes by the *Akagi*'s fighter group, which added to the personnel casualties. By the end of the attack, of the 55 bombers on base, five B-17s, seven B-18s, and two A-20s were destroyed, and another 19 damaged. Only 22 bombers remained intact.

To complete the already extensive damage to Kaneohe Naval Air Station, 18 horizontal bombers from *Shokaku* began their attack at 0855hrs. The principal targets were the hangars on the south side of the airfield. Hangar Number 1 was hit and the resulting fire destroyed the four PBYs inside. Eight *Hiryu* fighters swooped in to complete the destruction. After a single pass, they moved south to Bellows Field. At 0905hrs, nine *Soryu* fighters arrived and six commenced strafing attacks. During this attack, the leader of the *Soryu* fighter group was hit and eventually crashed. Of all the airfields on the island, Kaneohe suffered the most. Bombs destroyed two hangars and 27 aircraft were destroyed with the remaining six damaged. This accounted for every aircraft present.

This panoramic view of Pearl Harbor was taken during the attack of the second wave. The photograph looks southwesterly from the hills behind the harbor. The large column of smoke in the lower-right center is from the burning *Arizona*. The smoke further to the left is from the destroyers *Shaw*, *Cassin*, and *Downes* burning in the dry docks at the Navy Yard. The intensity of the antiaircraft fire speaks to the speed of the American recovery. The heavy smoke over the harbor and the intensity of the fire may explain the relatively meager successes of the second-wave dive-bombers that had to dive into this maelstrom. (Naval History and Heritage Command)

Despite damage to many of the hangars at Hickam Field, many of the aircraft present survived the attack. This shows one of the badly damaged hangars with a B-18 bomber inside. In the right foreground is a machine-gun emplacement hastily prepared in a bomb crater. (Naval History and Heritage Command)

The third midget submarine was not recovered until 1960. This photo was taken on July 28, 1960 when the submarine was recovered near the entrance to the harbor. Both torpedoes were still aboard when discovered. (Naval History and Heritage Command)

**DECEMBER 7 1941**

**0900hrs Bellows Field attacked**

Wheeler Field suffered little from the second wave. None of the level bombers from *Shokaku* and *Zuikaku* were slated to attack this facility. Wheeler was a secondary target for fighter aircraft which had ammunition remaining after attacking other airfields. The *Soryu* fighters that attacked Kaneohe were moving to attack Wheeler when they ran into American fighters from Haleiwa; they never made it to Wheeler. At 0915hrs seven *Kaga* fighters made a strafing pass on their way north. This was followed at 0930hrs by 16 *Kaga* dive-bombers which also strafed the field on their way north. This prompted the scramble of several P-40s with the results described below.

Bellows Field was not on the target list for the first attack wave. However, this did not stop a single fighter from *Shokaku*, which arrived at 0830hrs, from briefly strafing the tent area adjacent to the airfield. The only effect was to warn the Americans that a larger attack could be imminent and allow them time to disperse the 12 P-40 fighters from the 44th Pursuit Squadron and the nine O-47 observation aircraft from the 86th Observation Squadron that were present. The P-40s had had their armament removed the previous day for maintenance and cleaning. Ground crews furiously began to reinstall the weapons, but this was a lengthy process. By 0900hrs when eight fighters from *Hiryu* showed up, only three P-40 aircraft were ready. Two of these

attempted to take off but both were quickly destroyed by the Japanese fighters. In total, three groups of Type 0 fighters approached from the north and proceeded to strafe the field for about 15 minutes. Losses included the two P-40s in the process of taking off, one O-49, and the B-17C, which had arrived after diverting from Hickam at 0825hrs.

Ewa Mooring Mast Field was attacked again in the second wave. It was used as a rendezvous point for Japanese fighters after hitting their primary targets. If they had any remaining ammunition, they expended it at Ewa. Between 0910 and 0920hrs *Hiryu* fighters and *Akagi* dive-bombers strafed the base. They ran into heavy antiaircraft fire from machine guns salvaged from damaged and destroyed aircraft quickly set up by ground personnel. For these reasons, damage inflicted by the second-wave attackers was light. However, at the end of the raid, 33 of Ewa's 49 aircraft were damaged or destroyed. Among the destroyed aircraft were eight SB2U Vindicator and ten SBD Dauntless dive-bombers (out of 32 bombers), nine Wildcat fighters (out of 11), and all six utility aircraft. Fifteen more aircraft were damaged.

## The American Air Response

Amid the scenes of devastating attacks on American air installations on the island, there were instances of American fighters taking off and engaging the Japanese. On these limited occasions the inexperienced Americans did well, mainly because the Japanese fighters had already dispensed with accompanying their bombers and were focusing on conducting strafing attacks on airfields. This meant that when American fighters encountered Japanese bombers, they scored easily. The Hawaiian Air Force claimed ten (with another left unclaimed before the pilot responsible was killed) Japanese

**DECEMBER 7 1941**

**0902hrs Dive-bombers attack ships in harbor**

aircraft downed, with another four probable and two damaged. In return, four American fighters were shot down, one by friendly antiaircraft fire.

It has already been mentioned that Japanese fighters arrived at Bellows Field just as three P-40s from the 44th Pursuit Squadron were preparing to take off. One pilot was killed while mounting his aircraft; the second was shot down while lifting off, killing the pilot; the third was shot down minutes later but the pilot was only wounded. At about 0850hrs four P-36 fighters took off from Wheeler. They were told to fly southeast to Kaneohe to engage Japanese aircraft reported to be in the area. In the ensuing action against eight Japanese fighters, one P-36 was shot down, but the Americans claimed three Japanese fighters in return, though it appears only two claims were valid according to Japanese records. Two more P-36 fighters took off later from Wheeler and claimed a dive-bomber.

The most effective American response was mounted from Haleiwa Field. This was a dispersal field used for target practice and was unknown to the Japanese. On December 7 fighters of the 47th Pursuit Squadron were located at Haleiwa. By about 0830hrs, two pilots of the squadron had returned to the dispersal field by car and lifted off with the first two ready fighters. These pilots, Second Lieutenants George Welch and Kenneth Taylor, mounted the most effective American resistance of the day. Finding no Japanese aircraft over Wheeler, the two sped south to the vicinity of Ewa, where there were plenty of Japanese. Here Welch shot down an *Akagi* dive-bomber and claimed another from *Hiryu*, but it was able to return to its carrier. Taylor added to the score by destroying a *Hiryu* dive-bomber. A third P-40, piloted by Second Lieutenant John Dains, departed Haleiwa and scored an unconfirmed kill of a *Soryu* dive-bomber after chasing it to the north of Oahu. This was the first American kill of the war. All three pilots returned to Wheeler to re-arm. In their second sortie, Taylor and Welch mixed it up with a group of *Kaga* dive-bombers over Wheeler. Taylor shot down two, and Welch scored another dive-bomber followed by a *Kaga* fighter. On his third sortie of the day Dains was shot down in a P-36 by friendly fire near Wheeler. He was unable to make a formal claim for his earlier success, but other evidence confirms that he had indeed scored the first kill of the war.

By 0930hrs, some 25 fighters had scrambled from Wheeler, but they were too late to engage the departing Japanese. Two additional P-40s and two P-36 also departed Haleiwa, but did not attack the Japanese.

The offensive response of the Hawaiian Air Force was feeble. Commanders had no real idea where the Japanese had come from since the information from the Opana radar post never made it to proper command channels. The first reaction was made by four A-20 aircraft sent from Hickam Field at 1127hrs to search south of Oahu. These were joined by three more A-20s at 1300hrs. At 1140hrs two B-17D heavy bombers departed Hickam to continue the search to the south. After seeing nothing there, the flight commander took his section to the north. It is unknown how close he may have come to the Japanese. At 1330hrs, two B-18 aircraft resumed the search to the south. All told, 48 Hawaiian Air Force sorties were flown to search for the Japanese carriers.

The burned-out wreckage of a P-40 fighter near Hangar Number 4 at Wheeler Airfield. Of the 99 P-40 fighters present on the island before the attack, only 27 were operational at the end of the day. (Naval History and Heritage Command)

## The US Navy Response

At the start of the day, four VP-24 aircraft from Ford Island were active east of Oahu conducting joint training with submarines. This was in addition to the three aircraft from VP-14 active around the islands on security patrols. One of these assisted destroyer *Ward* in attacking a midget submarine during the early morning. Of 69 PBY patrol aircraft on the island, only 11 were operational by the end of the day, and this included the seven aircraft that were not caught on the ground during the attack.

Of the 18 *Enterprise* dive-bombers that reached Oahu that morning, by 1200hrs nine were located at Ford Island. Now refueled and fully armed, they departed at 1210hrs to search north of Oahu for the Japanese. Finding nothing, they returned at 1545hrs. Other searches that day by navy aircraft included six floatplanes and five JRS transports pressed into service as reconnaissance planes.

*Enterprise*, located west of Oahu, conducted flight operations throughout the day. In the afternoon, one Dauntless pilot reported sighting two Japanese carriers southeast of Oahu. In response, *Enterprise* launched a strike just before 1700hrs of 18 TBD-1 Devastator torpedo planes escorted by six SBD-2s with smoke generators and six F4F-3 fighters. Of course, they found nothing. The six fighters were ordered to land at Ford Island. Approaching Hickam at 2110hrs, four were shot down and three pilots killed.

The leading aircraft of the first wave arrived in the vicinity of the First Carrier Striking Force at about 0950hrs and immediately began their recovery. As this was occurring, at about 1000hrs, the last Japanese aircraft had made their attacks and all aircraft, including that of strike leader Fuchida, had headed north. By 1115hrs, aircraft of the second wave began their recovery and one hour later the last aircraft was aboard. Heavy seas made the recovery difficult, and according to one Japanese source, as many as 20 aircraft were forced to ditch or were thrown overboard after landing as a result of either irreparable battle damage or heavy landings. After the strike had been recovered, the combat air patrol also returned and the fleet took a heading of 330° at 26 knots to meet the tankers of the First Supply Group. The Hawaii operation was over.

# THE ACCOUNTING

OPPOSITE TOP: This aerial view of Battleship Row was taken on December 10, three days after the attack. Visible in the upper left is the sunken *California*. Left of center is *Maryland* (lightly damaged) with the capsized *Oklahoma* outboard. Below them is *Tennessee* (lightly damaged), with the sunken *West Virginia* outboard. At lower right is *Arizona* with its hull shattered by the explosion of its forward magazines. The harbor surface is covered in dark oil originating from the sunken battleships. (Naval History and Heritage Command)

**DECEMBER 7 1941**

**0905hrs Horizontal bombers attack Hickam Field**

## American Losses

American naval losses were heavy. Of the ships present, 18 were either sunk or damaged as described in the table below.

This table shows the minimal effect of the raid in overall material terms. Of the 18 ships sunk or damaged, only three failed to return to service. The most heavily damaged were the battleships, but even if none had been damaged they still would have not been suitable for front-line work against the Japanese. Exact American aircraft losses are difficult to determine. Though the figures provided by various official accounts differ, what is sure is that American air

### List of Ships Sunk or Damaged

| Ship | Type | Condition | Returned to service |
| --- | --- | --- | --- |
| *Arizona* | Battleship | Sunk | No |
| *Oklahoma* | Battleship | Sunk | No |
| *California* | Battleship | Sunk | Yes (January 1944) |
| *West Virginia* | Battleship | Sunk | Yes (July 1944) |
| *Tennessee* | Battleship | Light damage | Yes (February 1942) |
| *Maryland* | Battleship | Light damage | Yes (December 1941) |
| *Nevada* | Battleship | Moderate damage | Yes (June 1943) |
| *Pennsylvania* | Battleship | Light damage | Yes (December 1941) |
| *Helena* | Light cruiser | Heavy damage | Yes (September 1942) |
| *Raleigh* | Light cruiser | Heavy damage | Yes (July 1942) |
| *Honolulu* | Light cruiser | Light damage | Yes (December 1941) |
| *Shaw* | Destroyer | Moderate damage | Yes (June 1942) |
| *Cassin* | Destroyer | Heavy damage | Yes (Rebuilt 1944) |
| *Downes* | Destroyer | Heavy damage | Yes (Rebuilt 1944) |
| *Vestal* | Repair Ship | Light damage | Yes (February 1942) |
| *Curtiss* | Tender | Light damage | Yes (December 1941) |
| *Oglala* | Minelayer | Sunk | Yes (February 1944) |
| *Utah* | Training Ship | Sunk | No |

BELOW: This December 10 view is of the Navy Yard. In the upper center is the floating dry dock YFD-2 with the destroyer *Shaw*, whose bow was blown off. The torpedoed cruiser *Helena* has entered Dry Dock Number 2 for repairs, as seen in the center of the image. It was the first ship to use the newly constructed dock. Dry Dock Number 1 is visible below and still contains the lightly damaged battleship and the wrecked destroyers *Cassin* and *Downes*. (Naval History and Heritage Command)

power on Oahu was dealt a shattering blow and that the US was unable to mount a coherent defense or pose an offensive threat to the retreating Japanese carriers. Total losses were 97 navy and 77 army aircraft destroyed; 24 other army aircraft were later written off. US Navy and Marine losses were broken down into 13 fighters, 21 scout bombers, 46 patrol aircraft, two transports plus five others. The Hawaiian Air Force started the day with 234 aircraft of which 146 were operational. Of these, 77 were destroyed and only 83 left operational. Exact losses were four B-17, 12 B-18, two A-20, 32 P-40, 20 P-36, four P-26, and three others. Damaged aircraft included 81 fighters, six patrol aircraft, and 34 bombers. Of these, some 20 per cent were written off.

Of all the losses, those of personnel were the most grievous. Military casualties totaled 2,335 killed, including 2,008 navy personnel, 109 marines, and 218 army. Wounded came to 1,143 with 710 navy, 69 marines, and 364 army. Added to this casualty list was another 103 civilians, including 68 dead.

## Japanese Losses

In comparison, Japanese losses were low, and certainly lower than the Japanese themselves expected. Aircraft losses totaled 29, as seen in the table overleaf.

Having the advantage of surprise, the first attack wave suffered very little. The cost of crippling the Pacific Fleet's battle line was a mere five carrier attack planes.

| Japanese Aircraft Losses by Carrier and Type | | | |
|---|---|---|---|
| **Ship** | **Fighters** | **Carrier bombers** | **Carrier attack planes** |
| *Akagi* | 1 | 4 | 0 |
| *Kaga* | 4 | 6 | 5 |
| *Soryu* | 3 | 2 | 0 |
| *Hiryu* | 1 | 2 | 0 |
| *Shokaku* | 0 | 0 | 0 |
| *Zuikaku* | 0 | 1 | 0 |
| Totals | 9 | 15 | 5 |

The cost of the attack on the airfields was similarly cheap – one dive-bomber and three fighters. On top of this, 17 dive-bombers, 11 fighters, and at least 18 carrier attack planes were damaged. When the damaged aircraft are taken into account, the total of aircraft lost or damaged reached 55 – about a third of the 183 aircraft in the first wave.

Shown here is a Type 0 carrier fighter that crashed at Fort Kamehameha near Pearl Harbor during the attack. The fighter bore the tail code AI-154 and a single red band around the fuselage, which indicated that it was from *Akagi*'s air group. This was the only *Akagi* fighter lost in the attack and one of only nine overall. (Naval History and Heritage Command)

The volume of antiaircraft fire increased dramatically by the time the second wave appeared over its targets. Even the Japanese were impressed with the speed and volume of the American response. Of the second wave of 167 aircraft, 20 were lost (14 dive-bombers and six fighters) and 16 carrier attack planes, 41 carrier bombers, and eight fighters damaged for a total of 85 aircraft destroyed or damaged. The fact that this was about half of the second-wave attack force is testimony to the increasing powers of defense put up by the Americans.

The losses to the carrier attack planes were the most marginal due to the fact that they operated during the period of maximum surprise or because they bombed from altitude and were not exposed to light antiaircraft weaponry. Losses to the dive-bombers that had to penetrate through all types of antiaircraft fire were the heaviest. Watching the speed of the American response, Genda had already decided that if a third strike was to be conducted he would not commit the more vulnerable torpedo bombers. This left the burden entirely to the dive-bombers that had suffered heavily from the morning. These two factors would have meant any third attacks would have been much reduced in numbers. Added to the aircraft losses were the five midget submarines with their crew of ten. Total Japanese personnel losses were 55 men.

# ANALYSIS

## The Military Impact

On a larger level, the raid offered the Japanese few military benefits. The strategic goal of the attack was to provide the Japanese with the breathing space required to carry out their conquest of the southern resources areas. However, given the balance of force existing before the raid (with the Imperial Navy holding an edge in every category, and a marked edge in aircraft carriers), combined with geography where the Japanese held many islands in the Central Pacific, there is no way the US Pacific Fleet could have interfered in the Japanese conquest even if left unmolested.

It is common wisdom to state that the attack on Pearl Harbor crippled the US Pacific Fleet. This is patently untrue. Because the fleet's carriers were not present, none were sunk or damaged. This "crippled" fleet, reinforced by units from the Atlantic Fleet, launched a series of raids against Japanese positions in the Central Pacific (and even Japan) between February and April 1942, and in May, just five months after Pearl Harbor, engaged a Japanese invasion force in the Coral Sea and issued the Imperial Navy with its first strategic setback of the war. Only a month later the Pacific Fleet's carriers ambushed the First Carrier Striking Force and annihilated its four carriers at the battle of Midway. Yamamoto's bid to destroy the Pacific Fleet was unrealized at Pearl Harbor due to bad luck and timing, and at Midway was squandered due to a combination of overconfidence, bad planning, and sheer bad luck during the battle. After Midway, the Japanese never had another prospect of dealing the Pacific Fleet a blow that could be called decisive in any real sense.

A Type 99 carrier bomber being recovered from the harbor after the attack. The aircraft came from carrier *Kaga*. Dive-bomber losses were the most severe of any of the Japanese aircraft type since most were sustained in the second wave after the American defenses had recovered. (Naval History and Heritage Command)

DECEMBER 7
1941

0950hrs
First wave begins
recovery

The gains made by the Japanese at Pearl Harbor were virtually meaningless. The Imperial Navy succeeded in crippling the battle line of the Pacific Fleet, but given that the Japanese themselves had just clearly demonstrated the primacy of carrier air power, this devastation meant nothing in real terms. The battleships destroyed offered the Americans little military value. By June 1942 the Americans had assembled a force of seven battleships. These were seen by the new commander of the Pacific Fleet as so vulnerable that they were assigned secondary duties as the Americans were preparing to fight the entire weight of the Combined Fleet at Midway. These ships were too slow to operate with the carriers, and their vulnerability to torpedo damage had been decisively demonstrated. These ships did gain a measure of utility when the Americans began the long process of retaking islands – the battleships proved able platforms for providing gunfire support against the well-dug-in defenders. Several of the ships sunk at Pearl Harbor even had a last hurrah at the battle of Surigao Strait in October 1944 when they engaged a Japanese task force that included old Japanese battleships.

The attack was a strategic failure as shown by the fact that Yamamoto still had to put together a plan to complete the destruction of the Pacific Fleet – work unfinished at Pearl Harbor. This led to the Yamamoto-backed concept to attack Midway and draw the American fleet into battle. As he had at Pearl Harbor, Yamamoto threatened to resign if he didn't get his way. Again, the Naval General Staff relented, and again the result was disastrous. At Midway four of the Pearl Harbor carriers were destroyed by American carriers. The Japanese planning process at Midway by Yamamoto's Combined Fleet staff had some of the earmarks of the planning before Pearl Harbor with its wildly inaccurate strategic assumptions and lack of planning precision for operational and tactical details.

In the end, it did not matter what the result of the Japanese attack on Pearl Harbor was. The losses suffered by the Pacific Fleet were insignificant when placed on the overall context of American wartime naval production. During the war, the US Navy commissioned 18 fleet, nine light, and 77 escort carriers, eight battleships, 13 heavy and 33 light cruisers, 349 destroyers, 420 destroyer escorts, and 203 submarines. Given this, the American loss of every ship in Pearl Harbor on December 7, 1941 would not have mattered to the eventual outcome of the war.

The strategic conclusion must be that Pearl Harbor provided little military gain for the Japanese. The inescapable conclusion is that Yamamoto would have been in a much better situation had the Americans actually attempted to mount the kind of drive across the Central Pacific that the Japanese had been planning to counter for the last two decades. In this scenario, the old battleships of the Pacific Fleet, provided with inadequate air cover, would not have been sunk in harbor, allowing the majority of their crews to be rescued and the ships themselves to be salvaged, but would have been sunk at sea where personnel losses would have been probably higher and ships losses permanent. In any event the Pacific Fleet, even if untouched on December 7 and ordered to move immediately against the Japanese, could not have interfered with the Japanese invasion of the Dutch East Indies and Malaya. This was demonstrated later

during the war when the Americans attempted just that. In November 1943 an infinitely more powerful and prepared Pacific Fleet began its drive into the Central Pacific and took until October 1944 to reach the Philippines. Yamamoto's desire to gain time by a pre-emptive strike against the US Navy ultimately was as unnecessary as it was ill-considered.

## The Operational Level

At the operational and tactical levels, the attack on Pearl Harbor was successful, if meaningless strategically. In spite of all obstacles, the Imperial Navy had approached to within striking range of the most important American naval base in the Pacific and delivered a heavy blow while suffering only minor losses in return. This was achieved in spite of a plan that embraced excessive risk. Leading up to the attack, Yamamoto stated his desire to proceed no matter what the cost or risk. The plan succeeded only due to a series of blunders by the Americans, who above all did not believe the Japanese had the capability to open a war with an attack against Hawaii. This translated into a lack of battle readiness at every level, from lack of action after early indications of attack to poor damage control for fleet units suffering damage. These American weaknesses overshadowed any failing in Japanese planning. They negated demonstrable Japanese weaknesses during the attack in command and control, target prioritization and selection, and bombing accuracy. Had the Japanese faced an alert and active defense, the results would have been much different, and deficiencies in Japanese planning more apparent. The results of a poorly planned Japanese operation against an alert American defense can be seen clearly at Midway, where the Japanese managed to inflict significant losses, but paid dearly for their inadequate planning.

## The Follow-up Controversy

One of the persistent myths surrounding the Pearl Harbor attack is the Japanese failure to launch a third strike to destroy the facilities of the naval base itself. Such a strike, many reason, would have been even more valuable than attacking the fleet and would have forced the Americans to withdraw to the West Coast thus prolonging the war considerably. But while the Japanese were guilty of

This was the scene after the attackers departed. The view is looking toward Pearl Harbor from the Aiea area. *Nevada* can be seen in the center of the image. The large column of smoke to the left of it is from *Shaw* burning in the floating dry dock YFD-2. Battleship Row is in the right center with the heaviest smoke coming from *Arizona*. The destruction evident in this scene demonstrates that the Japanese had succeeded beyond their expectations with the exception of not having the opportunity to attack the American carriers. (Naval History and Heritage Command)

**DECEMBER 7 1941**

**1115hrs Second wave begins recovery**

several inaccurate assumptions during the planning of the attack, they are entirely blameless when it comes to any lack of a third strike.

The admirals of the Imperial Navy were steeped and trained in the classic tenets of sea control. This required them to engage the enemy fleet in a decisive battle, destroy that fleet, and then accrue the benefits of sea control enjoyed by the winner. This is what Yamamoto aimed to accomplish at Pearl Harbor. In this context it would have been inconceivable that the Japanese would have placed attacks on a naval facility on the same plane, or given it greater importance, as advocated by some, than attacking units of the Pacific Fleet.

Even if they had, there were many reasons why this could not have been done successfully. By the time the Japanese strike had returned to their carriers it was 1215hrs. Sunset on December 7 was at 1712hrs. Without prior planning, there was no possibility that the Japanese could have performed all the functions necessary to getting a major strike off – including debriefing and briefing air crew, and repairing and rearming all aircraft in the time allotted.

Current mythology has Fuchida returning from the strike and demanding that Nagumo order a third strike to attack the naval facilities. In fact, this was a story he invented in 1963 while retelling his account of the raid to American historian Gordon Prange. Nobody present on *Akagi* on the afternoon of the December 7 could recall any argument between Nagumo and Fuchida, and even Fuchida himself when he was interrogated after the war never mentioned such a debate. The fact of the matter was that Nagumo had accomplished his orders, inflicted heavy damage on the Americans while suffering surprisingly little damage to himself, and was very content to head for home secure in the knowledge he had scored a major victory. There was no debate on the matter. In any event, there was insufficient fuel for any other course of action.

It is only with the benefit of perfect hindsight that a third attack could even be considered possible. Nagumo was unclear as to the degree of damage he had caused to American air power and thus was vague as to the degree to which the Americans could strike back. Most importantly, he knew that no American carriers had been present in harbor. Before launching any additional strike, he would have had to search for the missing carriers and plan to deal with any remaining American land-based air power; this would have detracted from his ability to mount a large strike devoted solely to naval facilities.

Additionally, the amount of aircraft available for a third strike would not have been sufficient to guarantee decisive results, and would have been totally inadequate to deliver a knock-out blow to such a large target area as the Navy Yard and surrounding fuel tanks. It must be remembered that Fuchida had decided that the strength of the American defenses ruled out use of the vulnerable carrier attack planes. This left the dive-bombers to carry the load of any third strike. The First Carrier Striking Force embarked a total of 141 dive-bombers at the start of the attack. Of these, 15 had been lost and another 58 damaged (and this total is incomplete due to lack of records for *Hiryu*), which together accounted for over half of the beginning dive-bomber total. Undoubtedly, some of the reported damage could have been quickly repaired, but the bottom line is that the Japanese could not have mounted a third attack in great numbers. It also needs to be remembered that any third strike would have faced a fully alerted American defense, which, presumably, would have included radar-directed fighter interceptors. Based on the numbers of Japanese aircraft shot down or destroyed against the second wave, any third wave would have faced formidable opposition.

An area target such as a large naval base is very difficult to destroy. The only weapon available to the Japanese dive-bombers was the 250kg general-purpose bomb, which was far from ideal for such a role. Against pin-point targets, the highly trained Japanese dive-bomber aviators had an ability to deal punishing blows (though these same pilots had just shown hours earlier that they were largely unable to hit stationary ships). Against a large target, like the facilities at Pearl Harbor, the power of the First Carrier Striking Force was more limited. It is not possible that a relatively small number of bombs could have knocked out the base. This was demonstrated a few months later when a strike of some 70 Japanese dive- and horizontal bombers from four carriers failed to knock out even a single airfield on Midway Atoll. Even the large tank farms at Pearl Harbor were not a target easy to destroy. In Europe, such targets were only destroyed by multiple attacks by strategic bombers. Many of the 54 major fuel tanks at Pearl Harbor would have been hit in an attack, but the majority of the approximately 550,000 metric tons of fuel would have remained untouched. Any discussion of the effectiveness of a third strike also needs to consider the regenerative power of the Americans. Later in the war, the Americans proved their mastery in quickly building new bases or bringing shattered ports back to life. The matter of rebuilding a number of fuel tanks would have taken only weeks and could have been restocked with oil brought by a handful of tankers. On balance, the claims that the Japanese missed a strategic opportunity to knock out the naval base at Pearl Harbor are unfounded.

This view shows the Submarine Base (right center) and part of the fuel farms in October 1941. Among the 26 tanks visible are two that have been painted to resemble buildings. Other tanks appear to have been camouflaged to look like terrain features. This is a small portion of the naval base infrastructure. Nagumo's carriers could not have knocked out such a large facility. (Naval History and Heritage Command)

# CONCLUSION

To examine the Pearl Harbor attack in only military terms misses the point of this seminal event. Pearl Harbor was the central event of the Second World War as it brought the United States into the war in time to shape the outcome and guaranteed that the Americans would fight the war to the finish. This is the true legacy of Pearl Harbor. It is a legacy that survives until the present in the minds of many Americans, and persistently in the new generations of American leaders.

For Japan, the ultimate result was utter, if predictable, catastrophe. It went to war against the most powerful nation in the world with only an ill-defined notion of how it would defeat such a formidable enemy. There was no concept of a classic victory against the United States in which Japan could dictate peace terms. Rather, it was envisioned that a negotiated settlement would be possible once the Americans realized the futility of trying to pry Japan's new-found gains in the Pacific away from it. Essentially, Japanese martial ardor and Yamato spirit would substitute for the lack of resources between the two contestants and force the United States to acquiesce to a new order in the Western Pacific.

However flawed such war termination planning was, and there is little to suggest that this vague Japanese concept of victory was based on reality, what little hope there was of success rested on American war-weariness. The Pearl Harbor attack put to rest any prospect of a negotiated settlement by the Americans. Perhaps the American public would not be willing to risk never-ending casualties for Chinese sovereignty or to recover lost British colonies, but there was no price too high to pay to avenge Pearl Harbor. With the slogan "Remember Pearl Harbor" drilled into every American, there was little prospect that the United States would compromise on the outcome of the war.

The Japanese attack on Pearl Harbor relieved President Roosevelt of his concerns about taking the United States into the war. The day following the attack, the American Congress declared war on Japan and this was followed two days later with a declaration of war on Germany, after the

DECEMBER 7
1941

1215hrs
Last aircraft
recovered; First
Carrier Striking
Force heads
west

...we here highly resolve that these dead shall not have died in vain...

REMEMBER DEC. 7th!

The attack on Pearl Harbor, viewed by Americans as a sneak attack, proved to be a powerful rallying point as the United States geared up for total war. This poster issued in 1942 is an example. It featured a quotation from Abraham Lincoln's Gettysburg Address: " ... we here highly resolve that these dead shall not have died in vain ..." (Naval History and Heritage Command)

Germans had declared war on the United States in support of its Japanese allies. History will never know if and when the Americans would have responded to a Japanese attack solely against Dutch and British colonies, but it is clear that Roosevelt did not have the required level of support to take America to war in 1941 over such Japanese aggression. Thus the Pearl Harbor attack must be seen as the ultimate folly of a nation provoking a war against a much stronger opponent, which in the end all but guaranteed its defeat.

# BIBLIOGRAPHY

Aiken, David, *Torpedoing Pearl Harbor, Military History*, December 2001

Aiken, David, *Ghosts of Pearl Harbor, Flight Journal*, June 2007

Arakaki, Leatrice and Kuborn, John, *7 December 1941, The Air Force Story*, Pacific Air Forces Office of History: Hickam Air Force Base, Hawaii (1991)

Boyd, Carl and Yoshida, Akihiko, *The Japanese Submarine Force and World War II*, Naval Institute Press, Annapolis (1995)

Carpenter, Dorr and Polmar, Norman, *Submarines of the Imperial Japanese Navy*, Naval Institute Press, Annapolis (1986)

De Virgilio, John, *Japanese Thunderfish, Naval History*, Winter 1991

Dillon, Katherine and Goldstein, Donald, eds, *The Pearl Harbor Papers, Inside the Japanese Plans*, Brassey's, Washington, D.C. (1993)

Dillon, Katherine and Goldstein, Donald, eds, *The Pacific War Papers, Japanese Documents of World War II*, Potomac Books, Washington, D.C. (2004)

Dull, Paul, *A Battle History of the Imperial Japanese Navy*, Naval Institute Press, Annapolis (1978)

Evans, David, ed., *The Japanese Navy in World War II*, Naval Institute Press, Annapolis (1986)

Kimmett, Larry and Regis, Margaret, *The Attack on Pearl Harbor, An Illustrated History*, Navigator Publishing, Seattle (1992)

Kinzey, Bert, *Attack On Pearl Harbor*, Military Aviation Archives Publication, Virginia (2010)

Lord, Walter, *Day of Infamy*, Henry Holt and Company, New York (2001)

Lott, Arnold, and Sumrall, Robert, *USS Ward – The First Shot*, The First Shot Naval Vets, Minnesota (1983)

Madsen, Daniel, *Resurrection, Salvaging the Battle Fleet at Pearl Harbor*, Naval Institute Press, Annapolis (2003)

Maloney, Ed and Thorpe, Don, *Tora! Tora! Pearl Harbor*, Planes of Fame Publication, Corona del Mar, n.d.

McGovern, Terrance and Williford, Glen, *Defenses of Pearl Harbor and Oahu 1907–50*, Osprey, Oxford (2003)

Morison, Samuel Eliot, *The Rising Sun in the Pacific, 1931–April 1942*, Volume III in the *History of United States Naval Operations in World War II*, Little, Brown and Company, Boston (1975)

Peattie, Mark, *Sunburst, The Rise of Japanese Naval Air Power, 1909–1941*, Naval Institute Press, Annapolis (2001)

Prange, Gordon, *At Dawn We Slept*, McGraw-Hill, New York (1981)

Prange, Gordon, *Dec. 7 1941, The Day the Japanese Attacked Pearl Harbor*, Wings Books, New York (1991)

Record, Jeffrey, *A War It Was Always Going to Lose: Why Japan Attacked America in 1941*, Potomac Books, Washington, D.C. (2011)

Smith, Carl, *Pearl Harbor*, Osprey, Oxford (2001)

Stillwell, Paul, ed., *Air Raid: Pearl Harbor!: Recollections of a Day of Infamy*, Naval Institute Press, Annapolis (1981)

Werneth, Ron, *Beyond Pearl Harbor: The Untold Stories of Japan's Naval Airmen*, Schiffer, Pennsylvania (2008)

Willmott, H. P., *Pearl Harbor*, Sterling Publishing Co., New York (2001)

Zimm, Alan, *The Attack on Pearl Harbor, Strategy, Combat, Myths, Deceptions*, Casemate, Pennsylvania (2011)

The enduring image of the attack for most Americans is the USS *Arizona* Memorial in Pearl Harbor. It was built over the wreck of the sunken battleship and remains the most visited spot on Oahu since its dedication in 1962. (Naval History and Heritage Command)

# INDEX

Figures in bold refer to illustrations and maps